The Black Archive #26

THE

DÆMONS

By Matt Barber

Published December 2018 by Obverse Books

Cover Design © Cody Schell

Text © Matt Barber, 2018

Range Editors: Paul Simpson, Philip Purser-Hallard

With love and thanks to my parents, my brother and to Kristen for all their support and encouragement and to all the Blue Box Podcasters for keeping **Doctor Who** fresh for me. In particular thanks to JR Southall for the loan of so much research material, Lucy Hilliar and Professor Marion Gibson for witchcraft advice, Dylan Rees for the old magazines, and Paul Simpson for fine editing and vital **Doctor Who** fact checking.

Also Available

CONTENTS

OVERVIEW

Serial Title: *The Dæmons*

Writer: Guy Leopold (Barry Letts and Robert Sloman)

Director: Christopher Barry

Original UK Transmission Dates: 22 May – 19 June 1971

Running Time: Episode 1: 25m 05s

Episode 2: 24m 20s

Episode 3: 24m 27s

Episode 4: 24m 25s

Episode 5: 24m 04s

UK Viewing Figures: Episode 1: 9.2 million

Episode 2: 8.0 million

Episode 3: 8.1 million

Episode 4: 8.1 million

Episode 5: 8.3 million

Regular Cast: Jon Pertwee (The Doctor), Katy Manning (Jo Grant), Nicholas Courtney (Brigadier Lethbridge-Stewart), Roger Delgado (The Master), Richard Franklin (Captain Yates), John Levene (Sergeant Benton)

Guest Cast: Stephen Thorne (Azal), Stanley Mason (Bok), Damaris Hayman (Miss Hawthorne), Robin Wentworth (Prof Horner), David Simeon (Alastair Fergus), Alec Linstead (Sgt Osgood), Rollo Gamble (Winstanley), Don McKillop (Bert the Landlord), John Joyce (Garvin),

Jon Croft (Tom Girton), Matthew Corbett (Jones), James Snell (Harry), Christopher Wray (PC Groom), Eric Hillyard (Dr Reeves), John Owens (Thorpe), Gerald Taylor (Baker's Man), The Headington Quarry Men (Morris Dancers)

Antagonists: The Master, Azal

Novelisation: *Doctor Who and the Dæmons* by Barry Letts. **The Target Doctor Who Library** #65.

Responses:

'[*The Dæmons*] explores rich themes and imagery, takes Hammer horror tropes and an argument between science and magic, and turns it into a fantastic bout of family entertainment.'

[Andrew Blair, *Den of Geek*]

'At five parts, *The Dæmons* does suffer a bit from stagnation in the middle episodes, in which a lot of water is treaded as we wait for the climax in episode five.'

[Michael Hickerson, *Slice of Sci Fi*]

Production Code : JJJ

Synopsis

Episode 1

In the West Country village of Devil's End, a man dies after leaving the pub, the Cloven Hoof. The local white witch, **Olive Hawthorne**, is convinced he died of fright, and believes it is linked to excavations going on at the local burial mound, the Devil's Hump, led by **Professor Horner**. She heads to the Hump to try to stop the dig before death and destruction is rained on them all but gets nowhere with the rational Horner.

Jo Grant tries to get **the Doctor** to watch the BBC3 broadcast live from the dig, but his interest is only piqued when he hears the name of the village. What he sees on the programme convinces him that he and Jo need to stop the dig, and they race to the village in his car, Bessie, eventually arriving despite signposts being turned by elemental forces to misdirect them.

Miss Hawthorne wants to enlist the help of the new vicar, Mr Magister (in truth, **the Master**) but he is unwilling to assist. He is in fact the leader of a coven who meet in a cavern beneath the church, trying to raise **Azal** at the exact moment that Horner breaks into the Devil's Hump — and that the Doctor and Jo arrive in a last-ditch attempt to stop it. A huge blast kills Horner and leaves the Doctor apparently frozen to death.

Episode 2

Captain Yates and **Sergeant Benton** see the devastation at the dig on TV and use **the Brigadier**'s helicopter to fly down. After spotting giant hoofprints from the air, they find Jo looking after the unconscious Doctor in the Cloven Hoof.

8

Benton goes to investigate the tracks but hears cries for help from the church vestry, and lets Miss Hawthorne out of a chest that she's been put in by the verger, **Garvin**. Benton is attacked by elemental forces in the vestry allowing Garvin to capture him and Miss Hawthorne, but as the verger takes them from the church, he's vaporised by a giant unseen beast, allowing them to escape. The accompanying heatwave awakens the Doctor – just as the Master welcomes Azal.

The Brigadier arrives on the outskirts of the village to encounter a heat barrier sealing Devil's End from the outside world and tries to contact the Doctor. The Time Lord and Jo have returned to the dig, where the Doctor finds a tiny spaceship that weighs 750 tons. As he's explaining the world is in mortal danger, he and Jo are attacked by **Bok**, the gargoyle from the church, animated by the Master's will.

Episode 3

The Doctor uses an iron trowel and a Venusian lullaby to make Bok retreat, then he and Jo return to the pub. There he explains to Jo, Yates, Benton and Miss Hawthorne that they are dealing with Dæmons, inhabitants of the planet Damos, who resemble the Devil and have interfered at crucial points in Earth's history.

At the Master's bidding, **Squire Winstanley** gathers the villagers together. The Master tries to bend them to his will but they only believe in his power after he gets Bok to destroy the Squire.

Over the radio, the Doctor tells UNIT technician **Sergeant Osgood,** part of the Brigadier's team, to build a diathermic energy exchanger to deal with the barrier. When the sergeant fails to understand, the Doctor and Jo head out to meet him in Bessie to explain, unaware that one of the Master's minions has stolen the UNIT helicopter, and is intent on killing them. Yates follows to warn the Doctor.

The helicopter pilot tries to force the Doctor to drive into the barrier, but instead is destroyed himself. However, Jo is thrown out of Bessie during the chase, and Yates takes her back to the pub to recover.

While the Doctor clarifies his plan to Osgood, the Master summons Azal again. A fresh heat wave strikes as the Dæmon arrives – but the Master has underestimated his control of Azal and desperately tries to stop the Dæmon killing him.

Episode 4

The Master wants Azal to give him his power so the Time Lord can become this world's leader – but Azal is aware of the Doctor's presence on Earth, and wants to speak with him first. When Azal returns for the third and final time, it will be to pass on his power, or destroy the Earth entirely.

The Doctor realises time is getting short and becomes increasingly curt with Osgood as he explains his device yet another time. A groggy Jo has been woken by the arrival of Azal and gone to the cavern where Yates finds her. They hide as the coven arrives.

Bert, the pub landlord, has been spying for the Master, and now tries to shoot the Doctor as he drives back from the barrier, without success. However, as the Doctor walks by the maypole on the village green around which Morris dancers are congregating, he is captured by Bert and tied to the pole. The Doctor tries to persuade the villagers that the Master is their enemy, but Bert instead rallies them to burn the Doctor as a witch.

Just as the Doctor's immolation seems imminent, Miss Hawthorne comes out of the pub saying the Doctor is the great wizard Quiquaequod and encourages him to give the villagers a sign. Benton shoots at the targets the Doctor names, and the villagers are impressed, doubly so when the Doctor uses Bessie's remote control to run Bert down.

In the cavern, the Master calls Azal for the final time, preparing to kill a chicken as part of the ritual. This is too much for Jo, who bursts from hiding – as Azal arrives.

Episode 5

Mike tries to rescue Jo but is knocked out, as Jo is taken to be prepared for sacrifice. When he recovers consciousness, he stumbles from the church to tell the Doctor and Benton that the Master has their friend. The Doctor instructs the Brigadier that the machine has to come through immediately; finally, Osgood gets it working and the UNIT troops come through – but the machine itself explodes. The Doctor realises he must face Azal alone.

Azal has been affected by the machine's operation, but is recovering now it's been destroyed. The Doctor bluffs that he can destroy Azal, but the Dæmon sees through the lie. Azal isn't sure whether to complete his experiment by passing his power to the Master or to destroy Earth – but the Doctor offers a third alternative: leave humanity alone. Azal decides to pass his power to the Doctor, but that's the last thing the Doctor wants.

Trying to come to the Doctor's aid, the Brigadier, Yates and Benton face off against Bok, who resists all attacks.

The Doctor's refusal bemuses Azal, who decides to bequeath his power to the Master and eliminate the Doctor. Jo jumps in the way to stop Azal using a deadly bolt of energy, telling the Dæmon to kill her rather than the Doctor, who is a good man. This totally confuses Azal who self-destructs, taking the church with him.

The Master, the coven, the Doctor and Jo get out just in time, and the Master is captured by UNIT. As he's driven off to prison, the Doctor and Jo join Benton and Miss Hawthorne in a fertility dance around the maypole. Rather than join them the Brigadier and Yates decide to have a pint in the pub instead.

troduction: What is *The Dæmons*?

Viewed at the distance of 46 years, the final story of the eighth season of **Doctor Who** seems conventional, even middle-of-the-road. Many of the major components of the era are in place: it's a UNIT story set on Earth in the present day and features the Master played by Roger Delgado. There are motorbikes, helicopters, explosions, comedy yokels, car chases and fist-fights. It is notorious as a story beloved by the people who made it, as fan critic Stephen James Walker states:

> 'There is no denying [...] that it is a superbly written and extremely well made story that encapsulates perhaps better than any other the elements that combined to make the third Doctor's era such a popular and successful one.'[1]

This seemed to be the general consensus amongst fans, but as Walker was assessing the qualities of *The Dæmons* (1971), there was a simultaneous reassessment of the story taking place. *The Dæmons* suffered from an anti-Pertwee era backlash in the 1990s, spearheaded by Tat Wood's 1993 article 'Hai! Anxiety' and then sustained by Paul Cornell in articles and in the survey of the Pertwee stories in *The Discontinuity Guide*[2]. Despite this, since the late 1990s it has hovered remarkably consistently in the *Doctor Who Magazine* polls just outside of the top 20 stories from the

---

[1] Howe, David J, and Stephen James Walker, *Doctor Who The Handbook: The Third Doctor*, p94.
[2] Wood, Tat, 'Hai! Anxiety', *DreamWatch Bulletin* 115, July 1993; Cornell, Paul, Martin Day and Keith Topping, *The Discontinuity Guide*, pp108-65.

original series[3]. Regardless of the pulls of nostalgia from the production crew and the pushes of the later and more politically minded critics, *The Dæmons* has always been there, solidly, stubbornly, almost boringly popular. But these twin poles of adoration and criticism alone make *The Dæmons* interesting as a story.

Despite Walker's suggestion that *The Dæmons* is somehow an ur-text (a narrative template) for the Pertwee years, when watched in isolation (or with one eye on what we understand **Doctor Who** to be) the story is actually one of the least typical in the series' run. In almost every detail, *The Dæmons* subverts our expectations of what a **Doctor Who** story should be. Written by Barry Letts and Robert Sloman[4], the story draws from a mine of evocative source material from Dennis Wheatley to HP Lovecraft via John Wyndham and MR James. It also adopts and reflects the popular fringe beliefs at the time in the areas of witchcraft and the occult. It embraces ideas in the realm of 'Earth mysteries' and the pseudo-archaeology of Erich von Däniken. Like many **Doctor Who** stories that play with literary and historical sources (*The Talons of Weng-Chiang* (1977) for example), *The Dæmons* creates a narrative collage, cherry-picking from imagery, characters, tropes and textures and manipulating them in a way that serves the structural requirements of the series. Despite this manipulation, however, the source material is still evident and it should be possible to untangle, reveal and explore the different threads that make up the story.

---

[3] 27th in *Doctor Who Magazine (DWM)* #265 (1998), 22nd in *DWM* #413 (2009), and 25th in *DWM* #474 (2014).
[4] As producer, Letts could not write for his own programme; the story was credited to Letts' and Sloman's penname Guy Leopold.

My attraction to *The Dæmons* comes not from a directly nostalgic regard for the story (I was born five years after it was broadcast) but rather from an engagement with the story based on a combination of where I grew up and my academic background. In 2000 I completed an MA in the History and Literature of Witchcraft, a degree that gave me a good sense of both the reality and mythology of the subject from the 16th century to the modern day (everything from Shakespeare to **Buffy the Vampire Slayer** (1997-2003)). I then used the skills and knowledge I gained from this degree when tackling a PhD which focused on the mythologising of American politics in film and television.

Approaching *The Dæmons*, therefore, I have a number of advantages: I have had, and continue to have, a personal connection with a number of leading academics in the field of witchcraft studies whose work I draw on throughout this book. These include Professor Diane Purkiss (who taught me during the MA) and Professor Marion Gibson, a closet **Doctor Who** fan with whom I had a number of conversations about this Black Archive and who kindly gave me access to an advance copy of her latest book.

My PhD brought me into contact with a number of film and television academics, specifically Dr James Lyons with whom I discussed the validity of the 'folk horror' genre. It also gave me a good sense of how mythologies (such as witchcraft and the occult) feed on cultural platforms (such as television series) and how mythologies can be **shaped** by what is presented on screen. In short, the divisions between mythology, history, memory and culture are highly porous – often what we think of as legend turns out to be uncomfortably real, and vice versa.

There is something 'occult' about *The Dæmons*, beyond its fictional subject matter and source material. There are many things that are 'wrong' with *The Dæmons*: a **Doctor Who** story without time travel, with little science fiction and, debatably, an ambiguous approach to the existence of magic; a story in which the TARDIS does not appear and is not even mentioned. Wrongness infuses the story even down to its unusual number of episodes, archaic title and the baroque pseudonym adopted by Letts and Sloman. *The Dæmons* is not unique in this iconoclastic fracturing of the expectations of the series – *The Mind Robber* (1968) performed many of the same infractions including the five-episode length (albeit with the TARDIS being apparently destroyed in the first episode rather than absent throughout) – but unlike that story, whose iconoclasm was, in many ways, forced onto the production, *The Dæmons* does not have any reason for being different. Letts and Sloman write what they see as, and what has often been cited as, a traditional piece of **Doctor Who**, but the result contains little that characterises the series. I would argue that the atypical nature of the story, and the paradoxical subsequent regard for the story as somehow typical of a style and time of the series has its roots partially in the occult source material Letts and Sloman are influenced by.

The history of the occult is the history of a collision, sometimes a complex cooperation, between high and low culture. It's the conflict between kings and peasants; mainstream and populist academics; high-brow authors and pot-boiling hacks; genre cinema and arthouse.

The occult is what happens when the Apollonian meets the Dionysian; when Ben Jonson's courtly and urbane *Masque of Queens* (1609) meets Ford, Dekker and Rowley's schlocky and

16

urban *The Witch of Edmonton* (1621). In more recent times it's the distinction between Keith Thomas and Margaret Murray; Aleister Crowley and Gerald Gardner; the Doctor, the Master and Miss Hawthorne.

The conflict is at the heart of the paradox in the career of MR James, a renowned academic by day, an ephemeral ghost story writer by night, but only remembered for his work as the latter. The conflict is the source of the aggrandised self-perception of author Dennis Wheatley, a man who thought he was exposing the truth of a dark conspiracy but was really just writing pulp fiction perfect for adaptation and pastiche.

But it isn't just about binary oppositions. The occult is often a fusion or a reconciliation of the culturally high and low; of the politically left and right; of science and magic. It's what occupies the liminal space between the elite and the popular; colonising the vacuum that remains when the rational tendencies of society erodes the religious structures.

It is what happens when the Master uses science to raise the Devil, and the Doctor works with a witch to defeat him. Science and magic; modernism and paganism – themes that don't just set up oppositions within *The Dæmons*, but blur together so, by the end, as he performs an ancient fertility dance, the Doctor acknowledges (maybe ironically, but maybe sincerely) that 'there is magic in the world after all'.

In this book, I will look closely at the cultural and historical sources for *The Dæmons*. Through these I will explore the foundations of modern witchcraft and Satanism as embodied in the story by the characters of Miss Hawthorne and Mr Magister. I will chart the rise of the New Age pagan religion of Wicca from a man called Aleister Crowley, a mountaineering Freemason dubbed by the national press as 'the wickedest man in the world' to a 1950s middle-class naturist commune in the New Forest[5]. I will explore the pseudo-historical work of Egyptologist Margaret Murray and priest turned modern witch-finder the Reverend Alphonsus Joseph-Mary Augustus Montague Summers (yes – that really was his name), two figures who, despite being denounced by academia, produced work that continue to define the popular cultural view of witchcraft and the occult in the present day.

After unpacking this historical (and not so historical) background material, I will go down a bit of a dark rabbit-hole exploring the cultural flipside of these theories. I will brave the purple prose of Dennis Wheatley, a man who turned his acquaintance and fascination with Crowley and Summers into a series of pulp thrillers, books that today could be best described as a collision between the pacing of Ian Fleming's **James Bond** novels and the occult conspiracy preoccupations of Dan Brown. I will spend some time examining the noir-ish pastoral horrors of John Wyndham, a novelist who was a founding father of the 'cosy catastrophe' genre and the apocalyptic Quatermass stories of Nigel Kneale[6]. Finally I'll go underground and look at the buried terrors of MR James and HP Lovecraft, whilst dipping briefly into the strange pseudo-archaeology of Erich von Däniken[7].

Through my consideration of Wyndham, Kneale, Lovecraft and

---

[5] Hutchinson, Roger, *Aleister Crowley: The Beast Demystified*, p17.
[6] Aldiss, Brian, *Billion Year Spree: The History of Science Fiction.*
[7] von Däniken, Erich, *Chariots of the Gods: Unsolved Mysteries of the Past.*

James, I want to see how *The Dæmons* can be positioned in the same genre as a cycle of movies that writer Mark Gatiss, citing an interview with director Piers Haggard in his documentary series **A History of Horror** (2010), described as 'folk horror'. I will look at how the themes and style of *The Dæmons* anticipate those of perhaps the grandfather of all folk horror, *The Wicker Man* (1973). I want to explore the ways the customs and structures of the English countryside and village are twisted and skewed in these films, and how this manipulation can be applied to *The Dæmons* to reveal complex political and social subtexts.

Finally, I want to explore the position of the story in the affections of fans today, how *The Dæmons* has bred spin-offs and reunions that revolve around the location of Aldbourne, the village in which it was filmed.

My goal with this book is to dig down into *The Dæmons*, to perform a piece of cultural archaeology on the story to expose the source material beneath the surface and then to explore how this source material at the time of the production of the story had wider implications. In doing so, I hope to demonstrate how such an innocuous seeming story has bewitched some areas of fandom, and become demonised by others.

Chapter 1: The Unholy Power of Olive Hawthorne

The Matriarch and the King

In April 1970, eight months before Letts and Sloman started writing *The Dæmons* under the pseudonym of Guy Leopold (a combination of the name of Sloman's son and Letts' middle name), *The Guardian* noted the rise of an interest in witchcraft in middle England. Journalist Peter Harvey reported that:

> 'Police and Churches are concerned at the growing popularity of black magic and witchcraft. Memberships of cults and covens – particularly in the Home Counties, the Cotswolds, and the West Country – are increasing.'[8]

Harvey cited a Labour MP called Gwilym Roberts (the concerns were enough to reach Westminster) who called for a ban on 'this evil business' after he had seen a television programme in which a man proclaimed himself to be 'King of the Witches'. The man was Alex Sanders, an occultist and founder of the Alexandrian tradition of the Neopagan religion of Wicca. In 1969, Sanders openly courted the press and media to promote himself and his beliefs, but these articles and stories chimed uneasily with the brutal murders in Los Angeles by the Manson acolytes.

For balance, Harvey also interviewed a witch (white, naturally) called Mrs Eleanor Bone, a prominent follower of Wicca and a vocal opponent of Sanders. She lived, rather prosaically, in Tooting Bec

---

[8] Harvey, Peter 'Growth of Black Magic Cults Gravely Worrying Churches and the Police,' *The Guardian*, 6 April 1970.

(an area of London that, for reasons that don't concern us here, is notorious for fans of **Doctor Who** of the 1970s). Bone was known, in contrast to Alex Sanders' self-moniker, as the 'Matriarch of British Witchcraft' and was initiated to the 'old religion' in the 1940s – one of many possible prototypes for Miss Hawthorne. In the interview she defended Wicca against the accusations of Roberts, but not denying the existence of black magic cults suggesting that 'all this devil worship rot is attracting the people to the wrong sort of coven, and they are parting with money.'[9]

So, it is clear that in the early 1970s when Letts and Sloman formed the idea for *The Dæmons* there were a number of conflicts going on. Firstly, in the popular imagination and the media there was an association between Wicca and devil worship, a consequence of a rash of films including *Rosemary's Baby* and *The Devil Rides Out* (both 1968). This, as historian Ronald Hutton notes, become a kind of counter-cultural preoccupation feeding into the prevailing anti-authority mood of the New Age, with cemeteries desecrated in Tottenham and Tunbridge Wells[10]. Secondly, there was a conflict in the witchcraft community itself, between the publicly visible self-promotion of Alex Sanders and the more private and reserved 'traditional' Wiccan community. These, as we shall see, are a set of conflicts that informs *The Dæmons*. The story is shaped by the blurring of the lines between witchcraft and Satanism, in the three-way battle between the dark superstition of the villagers, the lighter and more ambiguous practices of Miss Hawthorne and the obstinately rational science of the Doctor. The prurient media

---

[9] Harvey, 'Growth of Black Magic'.
[10] Hutton, Ronald, *The Triumph of the Moon*, p332.

attention embodied by the BBC3 team[11] draws on the second conflict between self-promoters like Professor Horner and those like Miss Hawthorne who believe that the secrets should stay buried, both literally in terms of the barrow and metaphorically in terms of the occult history of the village.

When *The Dæmons* was written, the public perception of the occult was a contradictory mixture of suspicion, prurient interest, social conservatism and liberated excitement, but it is with the idea of Eleanor Bone, a middle class, middle-aged, pragmatic lady living in Tooting Bec that we should really begin. *The Dæmons* contains a heady mixture of Satanism, murder, horror, and black magic, but without understanding the more innocent and prosaic origins of Miss Hawthorne and her white witchcraft we cannot begin to understand a story in which the Doctor finally comes to admit that there may be magic in the world after all.

The Road to Devil's End

When an unnatural wind whips across the Devil's End village green, and Constable Groom, possessed by a 'dæmonic' presence, appears to be about to stove Miss Hawthorne's head in with a rock, the white witch performs what resembles an 'exorcism'. As part of this ritual, Hawthorne brandishes, instead of the traditional crucifix, an ankh. This is an incidental detail included, according to the DVD information text, after input from the knowledgeable actress Damaris Hayman and Roger Delgado. The presence of an ancient Egyptian talisman is significant in the context of the sources Letts and Sloman draw on. First, it fits with the general de-

---

[11] BBC3 is a fictional television channel, the existence of which reflects the near future nature of the UNIT stories.

Christianisation of the story (the replacement of 'crypt' with 'cavern' for example). The second significance lies in the birth of the version of witchcraft that the writers depict Miss Hawthorne as inhabiting. This can be traced back, not to the witch trials of the 16th and 17th centuries, nor to the wise women who lived on the edges of villages and brewed herbal remedies for the locals, but to two books published by an anthropologist in 1921 and 1933. In *The Witch Cult in Western Europe* and *The Gods of the Witches*, Dr Margaret Alice Murray proposed the theory that witchcraft, rather than being the abhorrent superstitious practices of ill-educated women, was, in actuality, a religion that has been followed in an unbroken but covert set of ceremonies and beliefs since ancient Egypt and even earlier.

Born in 1862, Murray was an academic Egyptologist and an expert in ancient, pre-Christian religions. She was also a strong feminist and an active campaigner for female suffrage, at the time progressive stances fraught with danger. Her political views led her to examine the persecution of women in the witch hunts and to come up with an alternative to the consensus at the time that witchcraft was a delusion, a fabricated myth designed by those in power to persecute those on the margins. She built on Scottish social anthropologist James George Frazer's epic, multi-volume study of mythology and religion *The Golden Bough* (1925) but, as folklorist Jacqueline Simpson notes, Murray selected and adapted her sources to fit her theories and shoehorned in the material she focused on[12]. Her view was that witchcraft was, in the words of historian Ronald Hutton, 'a fertility cult focused on a horned god

---

[12] Simpson, Jacqueline, 'Margaret Murray: Who Believed Her and Why?' *Folklore* #105, 1994, p92.

who represented the generative powers of nature', a description that instantly suggests major narrative elements of *The Dæmons*[13]. This idea of a female-centric, organised pagan cult (albeit one that revolved around a male deity) proved to be an extremely popular one and Murray was lauded, becoming regarded as an expert on the subject.

Most of Murray's theories were, in the judgement of historians writing after the Second World War, based on little evidence and much conjecture. Published in 1971 (too late to be a direct influence on *The Dæmons*), Keith Thomas's monumental and still highly regarded study of the history of the occult, *Religion and the Decline of Magic* (1971) was at the centre of a resurgence in the discipline that included historians and folklorists such as Hugh Trevor-Roper, Alan MacFarlane and Christina Larner[14]. These individuals wrote studies that formed the bedrock of the modern historical study of witchcraft, jettisoning preconceptions and returning to a basis of hard evidence rather than conjecture. As such, Thomas's study dismantled Murray's theory in short shrift, framing her ideas as attractive but fatally flawed. His approach to Murray was brutal and curt, but there was a reason why Thomas felt the need to critique her so sharply. In 1929, Murray was recruited to write the entry on witchcraft in the *Encyclopaedia Britannica*, a key information resource for the general public.

---

[13] Hutton, *The Triumph of the Moon*, p195.
[14] Thomas, Keith, *Religion and the Decline of Magic*; Larner, Christina, *Enemies of God: The Witch-Hunt in Scotland* (1981), Macfarlane, Alan, *Witchcraft in Tudor and Stuart England* (1970); Trevor-Roper, Hugh, *The European Witch-craze of the Sixteenth and Seventeenth Centuries* (1968).

Understandably this essay was laden with her idiosyncratic theories and it survived in later editions until 1969 – by which time two or more generations, and a future generation (including myself as a child reading my parent's old copy of the *Britannica*), had happily and uncritically accepted her views. Murray's pseudo-folkloric theories were, as such, 'accessible to journalists, film-makers, popular novelists and thriller writers, who adopted them enthusiastically'[15]. To that list it is tempting to add 'writers of popular television telefantasy', as it is obvious from *The Dæmons* that Murray's ideas (or at least half-digested, second-hand versions of Murray's ideas) were central to Letts and Sloman's approach to the subject. Whilst they serve as a foundation for many depictions of witchcraft in popular culture, however, Murray's views on witchcraft are rarely taken-up wholesale without a degree of adjustment or dramatisation. Miss Hawthorne, the village witch in *The Dæmons*, is clearly heavily influenced by Murray but the character's practical, pragmatic approach to her position in the village owes more to the transformation of Murray's ideas into a new, semi-structured religion by a man called Gerald Brosseau Gardner.

Gardner was born 20 years after Murray and spent his, relatively mundane, working life abroad in Ceylon, North Borneo and Malaya. Through his travels, and in his spare time, he amassed a wealth of experience in esoteric philosophies and societies including tribal animism, spiritualism, Freemasonry, Co-Masonry (a kind of unisex version of Freemasonry), the Fellowship of Crotona, the Ordo Templi Orientis, the Folk-Lore Society, the Ancient Druid Order and

---

[15] Simpson, 'Margaret Murray'.

the Order of Woodcraft Chivalry[16]. When he retired he turned his hand to religion creation. In the Home Counties, Gardner encountered a wealthy elderly lady named Dorothy Clutterbuck who initiated him into the 'old religion' envisaged by Murray. Clutterbuck, according to Gardner, had connections with practising covens throughout the country and was involved in the notorious 'Operation Cone of Power', an attempt by the occult community to fight Hitler and protect Britain during the Second World War using defensive magic previously employed against Napoleon[17]. Gardner then began to document his experiences and the anecdotes of the witches he met, first in the form of romantic fiction in the novel *High Magic's Aid* in 1949 and then in 1954 and 1959 in a series of articles and books including *Witchcraft Today* and *The Meaning of Witchcraft*, studies of modern witchcraft that outlined the ceremonies and rituals of what Gardner called 'Wicca'.

In essence, Gardner took the academic work of Murray and Frazer and created a romantic and appealing work of fan fiction out of them (high and low culture combining again). This fan fiction gradually merged with Gardner's experiences of encounters with the various occult groups and began to turn into a mythology: a kind of historical-fictional hybrid with such porous barriers separating the reality and fantasy that it has challenged subsequent historians, and even Wiccan adherents, to define where Gardiner's desires and invention ended and where what there was of truth began. Gardner compiled a grimoire called *Ye Bok of Ye Art Magical*, a fragmentary compendium of rituals, spells and ceremonies harvested from the different people he had met and from his own

---

[16] Hutton, *The Triumph of the Moon*, p239.
[17] Hutton, *The Triumph of the Moon*, p208.

imagination[18]. It has been alleged that this founding text of Wicca was, in reality, constructed as an exhibit for the museum that Gardiner would later build, and, given his history of self-promotion and the subsequent positioning of the book at the centre of the museum, it is tempting to think this may be the case[19]. The book was designed to seem old and mysterious. Gardner used an old leather cover, wrote in ornate script and used odd spellings, possibly to give the text an ancient and archaic aura. If *High Magic's Aid* was the Wiccan version of the Old Testament and *Ye Bok* was the equivalent of the Dead Sea Scrolls, *Witchcraft Today* was Wicca's New Testament, a book that took the fiction, unpacked the mythology and presented it in the context of the contemporary world.

Gardner trod an uneasy path between being a zealous and charismatic founder of a religion and a self-promoting charlatan, although historically the lines between these two perceptions are never clear. He was a self-publicist but also someone who understood how to shroud himself within a mythology. What started out as a scattered and incoherent set of societies and secretive organisations, Wicca has now become a religion that can almost be described as 'mainstream'. There is an obvious tension here between the appeal of the hidden origins of Gardner's religion and the open popularity it achieved. Perhaps appropriately for the writings of a naturist, part of the attraction to Gardner's work is in

---

[18] Whether the title of *Ye Bok* was an influence on the naming of the gargoyle in *The Dæmons* is not known. Given the obscure nature of Gardner's text, it's likely just a coincidence.

[19] Heselton, Philip, *Witchfather: A Life of Gerald Gardner vol 2*, p376.

the way it manages to expose and conceal at the same time; to retain the feeling of the secret and exotic mystery of Wicca whilst bringing it into the foreground. This conflict between the romance of the hidden and the desire to 'evangelise' the new religion reached a peak in the late 1960s and early 1970s with Alex Sanders and his radical reinterpretation of Gardnerian Wicca. Sanders was adept at promoting Wicca through the media, appearing in sensational newspaper articles, at public speaking events and on the television in 'King of the Witches'. Originally he was initiated into a Gardnerian coven but soon split with Gardner's philosophies by introducing more ceremonial and sexual components to the religion. The result of this schism and the publicity that went along with it made Sanders a far more prominent front for Wicca and a more likely source for the myriad of cultural recreations of it.

As with the wider occult world, there is a curious tension between the high and low cultural aspects of Wicca. It is a secretive cult that somehow embodies elitism and openness: elite because of its framework of pseudo-archaic texts and ceremonies; open because of the way it is constructed as a socialist faith. This tension is the key to its success, to the attributes that made it stand out from the pseudo-freemasonry of the occult societies that preceded it, and explains much about how it is depicted in **Doctor Who**.

Which Witch is Which in *The Dæmons*?

There is one clear character in Letts and Sloman's script that forms the centre of their notion of witchcraft in *The Dæmons* and that is Olive Hawthorne, so let's follow her through the story.

Hawthorne is a self-styled white witch along the lines of Murray; indeed at times she appears to resemble how Murray's own personality comes across in her writing: forthright, intelligent and eccentric. This 'sturdy rationalism'[20], mixed with a kind of pragmatic and flexible spiritualism, is something that is clear in Hawthorne's character from the beginning as she encounters, and argues with, four distinct characters: Dr Reeves, the local GP; Professor Horner, the visiting archaeologist; PC Groom; and, finally, the Master disguised as the Reverend Magister. Miss Hawthorne is shown campaigning against, as she sees it, Horner's ill-advised televised dig at a local barrow. She is shown ominously prophesying destruction, using the death of a local man as a portent. She is shown using an incantation to calm a preternatural storm as PC Groom, psychically controlled by outside (perhaps occult) forces, attempts to murder her. Finally, her (as it turns out, astute) predictions bring her to the attention of Magister, who orders an acolyte to kidnap her.

We find out little about the actual details of Hawthorne's life in these scenes, and indeed little more as the story progresses. We don't know where she lives, her social standing in the village is unclear, and there is nothing about her past. This isn't unusual in **Doctor Who** in which characters are often cyphers, broadly painted types rather than individuals with a backstory. With Miss Hawthorne, however, this lack of clarity actually complements her role in *The Dæmons*. Hawthorne is a liminal character, a figure both on the edges of the village and positioned on the edges of the narrative of *The Dæmons* itself. It is telling that the four encounters she has in the first episode are all with men who hold positions of different kinds of authority in the community: Reeves is the local medic, presented as a rational man of science whilst Groom

---

[20] Simpson, 'Margaret Murray'.

represents the law. Then there are the two outsiders: Horner is a pragmatic academic with little time for superstition, whilst Mr Magister, the villain of the piece, represents a corruption of the spiritual side of the village.

The sketching of Hawthorne is economical here: we know she is unmarried; she seems, by her accent, to be upper-middle class but off-kilter, like an EF Benson character[21]. As with Benson's comic village eccentrics, Hawthorne is depicted as an unmarried 'busybody', a thorn in the side of the hierarchy of Devil's End. In her conversations with three out of the four men she argues against rationalism and, in each case she is patronised and, in the case of the Reverend Magister, almost hypnotised. Reeves, Horner and Magister all fetishise rationalism and modernity: Reeves uses explicit medical terms to counter her claim that a man died of 'fright', Horner demonstrates a savvy knowledge of self-promotion in his decision to crack open the barrow at Beltane, whilst Magister describes himself as a rational man who views the world existentially. In short, Hawthorne is the perfect Gardnerian/Murray witch: on the edge of the village and yet central; irrational and yet, as demonstrated by her near death experience at the hands of a possessed PC Groom, correct. How then does Hawthorne's introduction in the story match the traditional and modern view of a witch and, crucially, what is missing from this depiction?

The stereotypical witch, as Diane Purkiss suggests, is a woman who lives on the edge of the village, who acts primarily as a healer

---

[21] Benson wrote the *Mapp and Lucia* series: six novels set in the 1920s and 1930s focusing on the social rivalries amongst the genteel upper middle classes.

alongside (or perhaps against) the local professional medics[22]. In short, a witch is a person who draws on inherited knowledge or personal, direct experience rather than authorised information to help (sometimes hinder) the lives of individuals. A witch is someone who challenges authority. It is possible to see Miss Hawthorne, in these four scenes, as fitting this bill. Importantly, Hawthorne is not marginalised by where she lives in the village, indeed, going by the scenes in the first episode, she appears to be omnipresent throughout Devil's End. Hawthorne's liminality, her **on the edge-ness**, instead comes from her knowing the truth about the danger the village faces and the men she faces patronisingly dismissing her, and uncomfortably, as we shall see, this continues when she meets the Doctor. Her status as a witch, therefore comes as much from the ways she is marginalised within the narrative of *The Dæmons* as it does from the brief flashes of operative witchcraft we see her perform.

Operative witchcraft. This is a term that has some weight when considering the things Hawthorne **doesn't** do. Margaret Murray makes a distinction between two aspects of witchcraft. The first, 'Operative Witchcraft', refers to the incantations, charms and spells that are used (and she extends this definition to encompass all religion and religious liturgy and sacrament). The second, 'Ritual Witchcraft', she defines as the practice of the witchcraft religion that Hawthorne claims to belong to: the 'cult' part of the witch cult[23]. Hawthorne refers to operative witchcraft in the first episode and we even see her apparently using a spell to calm the 'dæmonic' hurricane that appears to control PC Groom. She mentions, in a

---

[22] Purkiss, Diane, *The Witch in History*, p7.
[23] Murray, Margaret, *The Witch Cult in Western Europe*, p11.

decoratively off-hand way, consulting the 'talisman of mercury', 'cast[ing] the runes'. She also explicitly foretells the rising of the Dæmon Azal by referring to 'the Prince of Evil; the Dark One; the Horned Beast'[24]. These references are clearly broad attempts by Letts and Sloman to rapidly define Hawthorne's character, but they also place her in only one aspect of witchcraft as constructed by Murray. There is no sense that Hawthorne is a part of a cult or even a broader religion; indeed she seems at times to be more Christian than the local vicar (perhaps not surprisingly given that the local vicar is, in reality, a malevolent, murderous renegade Time Lord with a penchant for hypnotism). This, interestingly, aligns Hawthorne most closely with Dion Fortune, a novelist, occultist and magician who predated Gardner, dying in 1946 well before his Wicca 'bibles' were written, but whose work heavily influenced modern pagan witchcraft all the same. Fortune, in the words of anthropologist Susan Greenwood, 'expounded an esoteric version of Christianity', an act that makes her sound very much like Miss Hawthorne in these opening scenes[25].

There is also no sense that Hawthorne is connected with any form of contemporary counter-culture. The atmosphere of Devil's End is curiously dated and lacking in the modernity we see in other stories of the time – the interiors are filled with dark wood panelling and leather in contrast with the white and chrome laboratories and industrial factories; organic as opposed to sterile. This fact becomes interesting when the Doctor, Jo and UNIT arrive later, and Hawthorne's character becomes an 'establishment' one, standing

---

[24] *The Dæmons* episode 1. All dialogue quotes are from *The Dæmons* unless otherwise stated.
[25] Greenwood, Susan, *Magic, Witchcraft and the Otherworld*, p5.

for the traditional values of the village be they occult or Christian, and viewing outsiders with suspicion. This is far from the Gardnerian, liberal, socialist presentation of witchcraft. Hawthorne's brand of witchcraft is, in Greenwood's terms, 'associated with the learned and elite rather than ordinary village folk'. In analogous terms, Hawthorne embodies the 'high church' rather than the 'low church' of witchcraft[26]. This is not to say, however, that the ritual witchcraft and the counter-cultural aspects of the witch cult are not represented in the story. Miss Hawthorne's apocalyptic sermonising against blind rationality is matched, and indeed built upon, in the first episode by scenes featuring the Doctor and Jo Grant.

Jo spends very little time with Miss Hawthorne in the story – her main role appears to be to draw the Doctor into the narrative, then to be a potential ritual victim of the Master and finally to be the 'model irrational human' prepared to sacrifice herself to save the Doctor and thus bringing Azal to an explosive suicide. In the first episode, it is Jo's interest in the New Age that sparks a conversation with the Doctor about science, rationality and magic, themes that dominate the story. She begins by referencing the 'Age of Aquarius', which she, rather superficially defines as 'the occult [...] the supernatural and all that magic bit'[27]. This feels like Letts speaking through his character. The co-writer and producer of *The Dæmons* was known to be fascinated by the esoteric, particularly evidenced in later stories that he was heavily involved in the writing of, such as *The Green Death* (1973), which featured communes and crystal healing, and *Planet of the Spiders* (1974), which had at its centre

---

[26] Greenwood, *Magic, Witchcraft*, p7.
[27] Episode 1.

Transcendental Meditation and Buddhism. There was a general new openness in the 1960s and 1970s to both work alongside and to fill the void left by the gradual decline of Anglican Christianity. As Greenwood states, 'the New Age [...] opened up the sphere of "mysticism"', of which magical practices are a part[28]. The interest shown by Jo Grant is, therefore, in keeping with the series and the wider society at the time; her attitude serves to paradoxically both work with and oppose the scenes with Hawthorne touring the village. The references to the New Age connect the 'traditional' witchcraft, derived from Murray via Dion Fortune, of Hawthorne with a broader set of contemporary and fashionable counter-cultural movements. Unlike Hawthorne's apocalyptic visions of the future, however, the New Age movement was built on, as theologian Paul Heelas describes, 'the idea that a significantly better way of life is dawning'[29]. The two approaches towards the occult from Hawthorne and Jo, therefore, have different sources, the former defensive, pessimistic and concerned about the future and about something being 'unearthed', the latter excited and keen to see what happens when Horner cracks the barrow open.

So Jo Grant and Miss Hawthorne serve to represent the twin poles of Wicca: the traditional and conservative and the young and contemporary. These are never entirely reconciled in the story, however, partially because the ritual magic of Mr Magister eclipses Miss Hawthorne's claims to be a witch and turns Jo into a victim of the occult rather than a proponent or explorer of it. The other person that casts both Jo and Hawthorne into the shade is the Doctor; his reactions to both characters expose an uncomfortable

---

[28] Greenwood, *Magic, Witchcraft*, p9.
[29] Heelas, Paul, *The New Age Movement*, p15.

misogyny within *The Dæmons*. This patronising isn't exclusive to this story – in **Doctor Who** throughout the 1960s and 1970s (and beyond) female characters are marginalised by both the narrative and by the lead character – but in *The Dæmons*, when considering how the story depicts modern witchcraft, this marginalisation takes on a new significance.

How Powerful is Miss Hawthorne?

The Doctor extols rationalism and science over superstition and magic. At first glance, in the context of the series, this seems entirely appropriate. The Doctor, particularly in his third incarnation, is explicitly presented as a scientist and as a mechanic: in his first season, for example, Pertwee spends almost as much time in overalls, hospital whites and spacesuits as he spends in his 'costume' of frilled shirts, velvet jackets and capes. The first scene featuring him and Jo in *The Dæmons* shows him tinkering with his car, Bessie, whilst Jo tries to interest him in the dig at Devil's End using references to New Age superstitions. The third Doctor is, perhaps more than any other version of the character, the least likely to accept or tolerate witchcraft and magic. This puts him at a disadvantage in *The Dæmons*. In this story in which magic and superstitious practices seem to have an effect, the third Doctor is out of his depth.

There are two things to think about here. The Doctor's explanations for the occurrences in Devil's End, and the role of the Doctor as compared with those of Miss Hawthorne and Jo, are worth examining. In each case, the Doctor perpetuates a kind of misogynistic attitude that connects him with a historical reaction to witchcraft both at the time of its persecution and at the time of the explosion of historical studies in the 1960s and 1970s.

The form of witchcraft that Miss Hawthorne embodies comes straight from Margaret Murray and connects with two main ideas: firstly that the witchcraft persecutions of the 16th and 17th centuries represented a male persecution of particular types of woman, who were 'burned alive by men who hated women' and became the victims of, in essence, a gender-driven Holocaust. Secondly Hawthorne's brand of witchcraft comes from the idea that there is in existence a modern witch cult, the origins of which stretch back to pre-Christian paganism, that takes the form of groups of women worshipping a female deity. Both of these ideas, whilst powerful and undeniably influential both in cultural and social contexts, have been shown to be myths. Historian Diane Purkiss makes this case in the first two chapters of her comprehensive and convincing study of the ways myths of witchcraft were constructed in the past and in the present, *The Witch in History* (1996), but in summary the persecution of witches, the 'witch-craze', was not as simple as it is presented above. To start with, many accusations were made by women rather than men; there is also no evidence that marginalised women were specifically targeted, whilst many women who were accused were in fact married and with families[30].

The view of modern pagan witchcraft as a feminist religion is also flawed. Undoubtedly, Wicca has at its core the writings of a woman, Margaret Murray, but she is recycling the work of men (including Jules Michelet and James George Frazer) and before her theories become a religion they were interpreted and filtered through the

---

[30] Purkiss, *The Witch in History*, pp7-8.

myth created by another man: Gerald Gardner[31]. Interestingly, whilst the notion of a Goddess worshipped by witches came from before Murray and after in the myth-making of Gardner, Murray herself posited a male God, a horned figure called Dianus. Whilst it has been successfully adopted as such, far from being a feminine religion, modern witchcraft has at its heart a number of men spinning the truth for their own ends with (mostly silent) women such as Dorothy Clutterbuck standing testimony for them. The male voice is also dominant in the academic studies of witchcraft at the time *The Dæmons* was made. Keith Thomas, perhaps the most influential historian working in the area, devotes only two pages to Murray and, curiously, begins by acknowledging her doctorate but then 'demotes' her to Miss Murray by the second page[32]. As Purkiss notes,

> 'Read as a grounding myth of identity, we might see the dismissal of Murray as the creation of a narrative in which the (male) truth of empirical history is opposed to the irrational fancies of a woman who cannot distance herself from the subject enough.'[33]

It is only much later that Murray was defended by folklorists and literary critics such as Simpson, Purkiss and Marion Gibson (indeed Gibson dedicates her most recent book to Murray alongside two other influential female academics). In the 1970s the voices describing, defining, adapting and mythologising witchcraft were male. Female voices were kept behind the scenes, drowned out or

---

[31] Michelet, Jules, *La Sorcière*; Frazer, James George, *The Golden Bough*.
[32] Thomas, *Religion and the Decline*, pp614-15.
[33] Purkiss, *The Witch in History*, p63.

reinterpreted by either dominant male historians or charismatic self-promoters like Gardner. The former targeted the 'irrationality' of the views of women like Murray, the latter celebrated it, but both groups of people worked to ensure that these views were kept in the background. Purkiss notes that:

> 'the whole discourse (however well-intentioned) thus supports the associations between the feminine and the primitive, the unspoken, the pre-historical, the material substratum of society upon which the (male) historian works.'[34]

The role of the Doctor in *The Dæmons* gives a different perspective. From the beginning, the Doctor is a combination of Keith Thomas and Gerald Gardner; of the historian who fetishises rationality and the charismatic investigator who is drawn to the occult mysteries of Devil's End. But there is something more complex going on in the story. Miss Hawthorne and Jo Grant, whilst framed as irrational and unscientific, are not without agency in the story, in fact, arguably, they are the only characters who are consistently shown to be correct. The Doctor spends much of the story unconscious, captured, or occupied with trying to find a way through the heat barrier that prevents UNIT from entering the village. He is shown constantly to fail, both in small and larger ways: he fails to stop Horner opening the barrow after failing to persuade the villagers to show him the way to the site; he fails to protect Jo when he rides Bessie perilously close to the barrier; his plan to get the heat exchanger through the barrier fails (following a miscommunication with the Brigadier) and, finally, his attempts to talk Azal out of

---

[34] Purkiss, *The Witch in History*, p66.

destroying the Earth fails. His only successes come with the actions of either Miss Hawthorne, for example when he is almost burned at the stake by the villagers and she convinces them that he is really a great wizard called Quiquaequod, or Jo, who ultimately causes Azal to self-destruct.

The Doctor isn't the only character to fail. Considering the complete lack of success of UNIT in this story, there is an irony to the Brigadier's story-long efforts to bring a squad of men to investigate the village. From the moment Miss Hawthorne pulls Sergeant Benton away from a cursed flagstone in the crypt of the church, to the now infamous failed attempt by the Brigadier and his men to destroy Bok, UNIT – the symbol of physical masculinity to match the Doctor's intellectual and rational masculinity – is shown to be impotent. In many other stories of this era, for example *Doctor Who and the Silurians* (1970) or *The Mind of Evil* (1971), the narrative is balanced between the Doctor thinking through a problem and the Brigadier blasting his way through it. In *The Dæmons* the narrative is, instead, balanced between the rational and the irrational; between science and magic.

We've seen this in the series since in stories such as *The Brain of Morbius* (1976), *Image of the Fendahl* (1977), *Meglos* and *State of Decay* (both 1980), to name just a few. What is different in *The Dæmons* is the fact that, over the course of the story, the irrational and the magical path, as followed by Hawthorne and Jo Grant, is shown to be the correct one, whilst the Doctor and UNIT are ineffective. The entire story, in fact, is one of women operating silently and subtly behind the scenes as the men strive to steal the limelight from the Magister's elaborate but ill-conceived ceremonies, through the Doctor's distracted attempts to gain the upper hand, to UNIT's ineffectual attempts to solve problems with technology and weapons. In this way, *The Dæmons* can be seen as a metaphor for the whole history and mythology of witchcraft.

Indeed it is possible to see a direct correlation between the presentation of female characters and the writing of Gerald Gardner. Gardner finds a balance between the concealment and revelation of witchcraft, his suppression and filtration of the voices of women (much like Letts and Sloman) serve paradoxically to highlight them. It is unarguable that **Doctor Who** in the 1970s struggled with the rise of feminism, and it is equally unarguable that there is a gender imbalance in *The Dæmons* both behind the scenes (the story is written, script-edited, directed and produced by men) and in front of the camera (2 female characters versus 20 credited male characters). In this imbalance, however, exists a parallel with the occult power of the women in Gardner's witch religion; in short, in *The Dæmons*, there is **a power in the silence** of the female characters. Whilst the men get the bulk of the dialogue, it is as empty as that of the pabulum of the news reporter Alastair Fergus. The men in *The Dæmons* are limited to incantations, technobabble and military orders, but, with the exception of the Doctor's use of a Venusian lullaby to ward off Bok, each fail: the incantations (in fact 'Mary had a Little Lamb' spoken backwards) lead to the Master becoming a victim, the technobabble leads to the failure by UNIT and the Doctor to fully breach the heat shield, whilst the military orders ('chap with the wings, five round rapid') famously leads to a puncturing of the pomposity of the Brigadier. Compare these to Hawthorne's relative success with words: her calming of the magical storm with a spell and her conning of the villagers during the Morris men stake burning attempt.

This is perhaps best considered in the context of other depictions of witches in the series – in fact, two of the stories mentioned above: *The Brain of Morbius* and *Image of the Fendahl* feature recognisable witch figures who are treated in entirely different ways to Miss Hawthorne. In *Morbius*, the Doctor encounters a female coven on the planet Karn. Unlike the rational men employing science and technology that had previously been depicted in the series in stories such as *The War Games* (1969) and *The Three Doctors* (1972-3), this cult, the 'Sisterhood of Karn', use what can only be described as magic, a mixture of ritual and incantation, even at one point attempting to sacrifice the Doctor to reinvigorate their sacred flame of eternal life. Whilst alien, the Sisterhood are explicitly drawn as stereotypical witches: grouped into a coven and using spells to affect the physical world. Two seasons later, in *Fendahl*, another witch stereotype is presented, this time more prosaically in the form of Ma Tyler, an elderly woman whose childhood proximity to a time fissure has gifted her with second sight.

These two depictions offer two aspects of witchcraft: the sinister cult wielding power and the rural wise woman offering support to her community, both of which are present (in one form or another) in *The Dæmons*, but the differences lie in the way the characters are shown to have power and the results of their magic. The Sisterhood of Karn are shown to be witches with a real and visible power: they are able to teleport and see into the future all apparently through chanting. They are also effectively immortal using a potion. In the smaller context of the events of the story, they seem to have power, limiting Solon's attempts to resurrect the Time Lord, Morbius; healing Sarah Jane Smith; and trapping the

41

Doctor. In the larger context, however, the real power comes from the Doctor and his practical, pragmatic approach to the dramatic events on Karn. In the last episode, the Sisterhood turn into the equivalent of the rural torch-bearing villagers from James Whale's 1931 adaptation of *Frankenstein*. Their problem with their slowly depleting 'elixir of life', the potion that gives them immortality, is solved by the Doctor's use of a strategically placed firework.

Ma Tyler has a kind of power as well, although less dramatic as the Sisterhood. In his Black Archive examining *Image of the Fendahl*, Simon Bucher-Jones considers Ma Tyler in the context of a long line of rural characters in 1970s **Doctor Who**, including the villagers of Devil's End[35]. It is true that the depiction of rural and working class characters in many of the stories produced by Barry Letts, for example *The Claws of Axos* (1971) or *The Green Death,* was cyphered and stereotyped, from Pigbin Josh to Dai Evans. This is in line with the methodology of **The Avengers** (1961-69), the series that provided a major influence on **Doctor Who** at the time by offering a strange, otherworldly pastoral construction of the England. *The Dæmons*, particularly in the depiction of Miss Hawthorne (admittedly not with the other villagers), departs from this, ironically considering the story drew heavily on the 1969 **Avengers** episode called *Thingumajig*, a story which opens with an archaeological dig under a church and the death of the archaeologist.

The influence of **The Avengers** in general does have far reaching consequences in *The Dæmons*, but in the specific case of Miss

---

[35] Bucher-Jones, Simon, *The Black Archive #5: Image of the Fendahl*, p110.

Hawthorne, she is not the outlandish caricature that Ma Tyler embodies. Tyler spends the story threatening the baddies with curses, reading the tarot, offering wise-woman wisdom and chastising her grandson over not using the best china when serving tea. All these (aside from the tea) are traditional aspects of the stereotype witch: cursing, fortune telling and protection from evil. Tyler is presented as less cerebral and less bookish than Hawthorne and her accent marks her as being a part of the rural working class. She also has less agency in the story, despite the Doctor (in his fourth incarnation) being less patronising and combative towards her than he is towards Miss Hawthorne.

Crucially, though, Tyler and the Sisterhood of Karn are shown to be witches with actual power, the latter owing to their extra-terrestrial nature, the former owing to a childhood lived close to a weakness in the fabric of space and time[36]. In short, the preternatural power of the witches in these stories is explained, as the third Doctor obsessively preaches, by science, or at least advanced and alien science. Hawthorne doesn't display any preternatural ability, but her ability to intuit and the fact that she is uncannily correct in her predictions and warnings makes her a far more effective witch than Tyler or the Sisterhood, both of whom rely on the Doctor to explain or solve their mysteries.

This view of the witch as a victim or an alien is one seen throughout most of the series[37]. From Old Mother, the doomed wise-woman in *An Unearthly Child* (1963) to the Carrionites in *The Shakespeare Code* (2007), witches and witch-like characters in **Doctor Who** have

---

[36] *Image of the Fendahl*, episode 1.
[37] Those seen in the Cartmel era are exceptions: Lady Peinforte in *Silver Nemesis* (1988) and Morgaine in *Battlefield* (1989).

been superficially powerful but, in the end, are shown to be secondary to the rationality and science of the Doctor and his companions. Only in *The Dæmons* do we see the reverse: a witch who appears to be deluded, but who ultimately is revealed to be the one person in Devil's End whose insight and intuition are consistently correct and who, by the end, is shown to be the most powerful character in the story.

'All That Magic Bit'

There was something in the air in 1971. The 'long 1960s', a period of immense cultural, technological and social change that stretched, according to some sociologists, from the birth of rock-and-roll in the mid-1950s to the birth of punk in the mid-1970s, had reached its apogee[38]. The United Kingdom had passed through the conventionality and social conservatism of the immediate post-war period and was inexorably tipping into postmodernism. Things began to fracture in the long 1960s: culture, religion, social groups, even countries began to break apart. Wicca was part of that fracturing, a new spiritual movement that, as a faith that had at its centre a strong feminist ideology, bridged the gap between youth culture and the establishment; between high and low culture and between politics and religion.

Into this context comes **Doctor Who**, a series that had, in the past, never been massively anti-establishment or cutting-edge but had always played with the zeitgeist, and fashioned eclectically ironic narratives from what it found in the world at the time it was made. Perhaps aside from Verity Lambert, the makers of the series had

---

[38] Agar, Jon 'What Happened in the Sixties?' *British Journal for the History of Science* 41, 2008.

always been somewhat establishment figures, career BBC men like Barry Letts, Terrance Dicks and Robert Holmes who, whilst being inventive and creative, drew on a mixture of sources from their own childhoods such as the Universal horror movies or B movies as their inspiration. The series was never strong at actively parodying or satirising the modern world, but in the depiction of witchcraft in *The Dæmons* goes surprisingly far towards tapping into the contemporary structures of, and sources for, Wicca. In fact, not only is the character of Miss Hawthorne a good reflection of the Murray and Gardner view of the witch, her role can be seen to actively interrogate the political and social debates surrounding the new religion. This is not necessarily intentional. In fact, given the nature of Pertwee's other stories, it is unlikely that Letts, Sloman or Dicks were somehow pushing for a progressive, feminist reading of modern witchcraft.

The series in the early 1970s is often accused of being establishment and conservative, and this accusation, whilst uncharitable, is not entirely without merit. But there is something about Letts' approach to the series that counters this. Letts was a combination of a free-spirited, liberal and spiritual man, and a canny, cultured BBC producer and writer. Under his guidance, the third Doctor, on the surface, was presented as a pompous, over-confident and intolerant alpha male, but, looking particularly at the stories written by Letts, a lot of this pomposity is amusingly punctured. The Doctor is still presented as a heroic character, and still finds the solution to problems, but along the way he is teased, affectionately ridiculed and, at times, proved to be misguided. This ironic presentation of the character reaches its zenith in Pertwee's final regular story *Planet of the Spiders*, written, like *The Dæmons*, by Robert Sloman and directed by Barry Letts. The climax of this story pivots on the third Doctor overreaching himself at the expense of his own life, in the words of Tat Wood, 'frail, scared and out of his depth'[39]. In retrospect, the Pertwee era is almost defined, not by a character who is flawlessly heroic and omniscient, but by one who is vulnerable and has gaps in his knowledge and memory. The five years are bookended by his desperate but futile attempts to save the Silurians in *The Silurians* and the parallel Earth in *Inferno* (1970), and his hubristic but enlightened death in *Planet of the Spiders*. *The Dæmons* forms part of this narrative, and Miss Hawthorne, a character who is defined by her inherited knowledge and uncanny wisdom, is a key to understanding and exposing the real flaws of the third Doctor.

---

[39] Wood, Tat, *About Time Volume 3 1970*-1974, p481.

Chapter 2: Satanism, Devilish Pacts and Scientists

In February 1969, the Reverend Ronald Adkins, rector of South Pool near Kingsbridge in Devon, found himself both in trouble with the Church authorities and in the national press. He was discovered, according to the article in *The Times*, in possession of material including letters that linked him with a black magician, an unfortunate connection that led to his being investigated by the Church[40]. The fate of the Reverend Adkins is not recorded, but his story is interesting on a number of levels. Firstly, there is something irresistibly exciting about the idea of an Anglican vicar, usually the mildest and most innocuous of religious figures, being involved in something as dark and mysterious as black magic. Secondly, the story highlights the renewal of interest in esoteric studies in the 1970s in academia and in the media.

Compare this story to others between 1968 and 1970. In 1968 Joseph de Havilland, a man who was apparently crucified without drawing blood, gave a lecture on the use of black magic to overcome pain, whilst in the summer of 1970, a Yorkshireman called Ronald Barratt died after participating in a Satanic ritual in a pub[41]. It is, frankly, unlikely that the Reverend Adkins was a Satanist in disguise, and more likely that he had an interest, whether professional or amateur, in the subject of the occult. It is equally unlikely that Mr de Havilland was really drawing on dark magic, or

---

[40] 'Rector Faces Black Magic Inquiry', *The Times,* 24 February 1969.
[41] 'Crucifixion Without Blood' *Daily Mail,* 10 September 1968; 'Man Died after Talk of Magic and Witchcraft' *The Guardian,* 18 August 1970.

that Mr Barrett's tragic evening in the pub was anything more than tragic hijinks ('I don't care what you say. The man died of fright!'[42]). Either way, Adkins' and Barrett's unfortunate stories and their appearance in the national press are a good starting point to a consideration of the state of, and interest in, Satanism and black magic in the late 1960s and early 1970s.

Aside from the evocative imagery of a Devon Anglican vicar potentially being a secret Satanist, it is the reason he gave for his letters that is really significant in the context of *The Dæmons*. A thirst for knowledge and the consequences of seeking too much knowledge are recurring themes in **Doctor Who** in the 1970s. They are also central to a number of the sources for Letts and Sloman's diabolic material, in particular *The Devil Rides Out* (1968), based on a 1934 book by Dennis Wheatley, and the myth of Doctor Faust. These two sources are joined by another: a modern-day Faust whose career and dubious hobbies provided a fertile reference point for villainous magicians in genre film, literature and television including Wheatley's villain from *The Devil Rides Out*: the 'great beast' Aleister Crowley.

In his study of fan culture, Henry Jenkins coined the term 'textual poachers' to describe the acquisitive relationship between fan culture and the narratives they draw upon for their fiction[43]. This term might also, at least in part, apply to the writers, script editors and producers of **Doctor Who.** The nature of the series, an anthology of independent stories that often draw (either as pastiche, homage or parody) from other texts and genres, has

---

[42] Miss Hawthorne, episode 1.
[43] Jenkins, Henry, *Textual Poachers: Television Fans and Participatory Culture.*

meant that often the creators of the stories have often emulated this fan approach. Selecting and modifying themes, images and tropes from literature, cinema, television and mythology, **Doctor Who** has retooled often adult oriented material for a family audience. In this chapter I want to explore how this approach to the adaptation of Wheatley and the Faust myth takes place and, specifically, how in *The Dæmons*, the characters of both the Doctor and his binary opposite, the Master, are shaped by the use of these poached sources. In doing so, I want to pull the veil off the surprisingly complex Faust myth, looking at how this plays with the notion of the 'scientist' through history. Finally I want to explore how the conspiratorial politics of Wheatley shaped **Doctor Who** in the 1970s.

Let's start at the beginning with Faust.

Signing the Pact

Over time there have been three main iterations of the Faust story, each nudging the story to different places: Christopher Marlowe's *The Tragical History of the Life and Death of Doctor Faustus* from 1604, Johann Wolfgang von Goethe's play *Faustus* from 1808 and Thomas Mann's novel *Doctor Faustus* from 1947. Each is based on an ur-text, a chapbook from 1587 called *Historia von D. Johann Fausten*, itself the fictionalised recounting of the life of a real man: magician, astrologer and alchemist Johann Georg Faust (born between 1466 and 1480, died around 1541). The perpetuation of the Faust myth is notable and perhaps explained by how the central story has been twisted and reshaped to suit the times. So the 16th-century chapbook presents the life of the magician according to the Protestant theology of Martin Luther, Marlowe's 17th-century play is concerned with the Counter-Reformation's 'war on secular hedonism and antinomian individualism: the reality of the terrors of hell, the immortality of the soul, and the possibility of eternal damnation', whilst Mann's novel reframes the story in the context of the rise of the Nazis and European fascism[44]. The story of Doctor Faustus and his unhealthy relationship with the Devil, therefore, is a perfectly malleable myth; Faust is a character-type that refreshingly regenerates to suit any time and any situation.

There are a number of common threads woven through all the retellings of the story, however; specifically a collision (and a state of confusion) between magic and science. Ian Watt, a social historian, describes the collective 'Faust' figure as:

> 'A bragging and unsavoury charlatan, no doubt; but also an unrepentant individualist who went his own way in a society where a regular job and a fixed abode were increasingly required. He united old and new traditions. The old is represented by his being called a conjuror; the verbal usages of a largely pre-scientific society habitually tolerated a now unthinkable latitude of meanings for conjuring, a latitude that extended from summoning devils out of hell to producing rabbits out of hats. But he was also an embodiment of the new forces making for change – the Renaissance humanists' revival of classical learning, for example, and their parallel pursuit of magical science.'[45]

The core Faust myth – an overreaching scientist who makes an

[44] Watt, Ian, *Myths of Modern Individualism: Faust, Don Quixote, Don Juan, Robinson Crusoe*, p40.
[45] Watt, *Myths of Modern Individualism*, pp10-11.

immoral or amoral bargain with a higher power – is an endlessly adaptable one, even when the science evolves over time from the alchemy and astrology of the 16th century, through the spiritualism and new occultism of the 19th century to the atomic and quantum physics of the 20th and 21st centuries. A way to unlock the mysteries of the Faust myth is this notion of magical science. Arthur C Clarke's third 'law' states that 'any sufficiently advanced technology is indistinguishable from magic'[46], and this ever-shifting notion of higher science is the key to understanding the character of not only the Master, but also the third Doctor. There are two sides to Faust: whilst he's usually perceived as a negative character, and his demonic flirtation is clearly at the centre of this, he is also, in many ways, the model of the modern man. Curious, progressive and ambitious, Faust can also been seen as a renaissance innovator, driven to advance humanity by turning to (and tackling) authoritarian higher powers. As Roslynn Haynes summarises:

> 'At one extreme, Faust may be regarded as an arrogant fool making a bad bargain with the wily Mephistopheles, who outwits him until he finally gets what he deserves. At the other extreme, Faust may be seen as embodying the noblest desire of man to transcend the limitations of the human condition and to extend his powers, for good as much as for evil, a Promethean figure who asserts the rights of man over a tyrannical order that seeks to enslave him.'[47]

This connects with the idea of the occult existing as a paradoxical

---

[46] Clarke, Arthur C, 'Clarke's Third Law on UFOs', *Science*, new ser, vol. 159, no 3812, 19 January 1968.

[47] Haynes, Roslynn D., *From Faust to Strangelove: Representations of the Scientist in Western Literature*, pp18-19.

relationship and conflict between high and low culture: the pot-boiling horror of the conjuror making a deal with the Devil butting up against the principled and self-sacrificing scientist, honourably, if single-mindedly, seeking higher knowledge. Writing about this contradictory nature of Faust, Inez Hedges notes that 'admiration, as well as condemnation, surrounds this popular, anti-establishment figure.'[48] This view raises an interesting possibility in the context of *The Dæmons*, and in the Pertwee stories in general.

Seen in retrospect, the Faust myth is the perfect lens through which to watch **Doctor Who**, specifically during this era. It is almost a cliché to describe Roger Delgado's version of the Master as charming, urbane and suave. A large part of this comes from Delgado's performance, but it is also embedded in the narrative of the series at the time. In his later appearances, through the 1980s and into the 21st-century series, the Master became a more traditional and, in terms of motivation, simpler villain. Peter Pratt and Anthony Ainley portrayed the character as either bent on direct revenge on the Doctor, or as a simply sadistic and power-hungry mad scientist. Even in the more nuanced and postmodern depictions of the 2000s, the Master and Missy are presented as insane and irrepressible mirrors of contemporary depictions of the Joker from the **Batman** franchise, playful anarchists defined by their personal relationship with the Doctor. Very rarely did the Master take on the role of Faust in these later stories. Delgado's Master, on the other hand, was regularly shown to be on a quest for knowledge, making unwise deals with aliens he thought he could control in return for enlightenment and power.

---

[48] Hedges, Inez, *Framing Faust*, p4.

The Delgado Master was, first and foremost, a businessman and an aggressive dealmaker. Consider his first appearance in *Terror of the Autons* (1971). The Master performs a hostile takeover of a company, his approach to the 'art of the deal' being rather unconventional and revolving around hypnotism and murder. Once at the top, the Master then uses business techniques to advance his plan: he forms an alliance with the Nestene Consciousness, reinvigorates a flagging research and development department at the plastics factory and then launches an aggressive direct marketing campaign. In short, the first appearance of the Master continues Robert Holmes' satire on industry by presenting him as the perfect CEO. The principal characteristic of the Master in these early stories is that of confidence in his own ability and his own dominance over others. And this continues. In *The Mind of Evil*, he poses as an entrepreneurial scientist who struggles, and ultimately fails, to control the evil-hungry creature at the heart of his Keller machine; in *The Claws of Axos*, he makes a bargain with the Axons in return for power but rapidly discovers that they are uncontrollable; whilst in *Colony in Space* (1971), he fails to make a deal with the leader of the Primitives. Bad deals form the backbone of every story in the eighth season.

So far, so 'an arrogant fool making a bad bargain with the wily Mephistopheles, who outwits him until he finally gets what he deserves', but no story in the eighth season comes as close to a direct acknowledgment of the Faust myth as does *The Dæmons*. In many respects, in terms of the characterisation of the Master, the final story of the season is a culmination of the others. Once again, the Master has insinuated himself into an organisation, and once again he is seeking an alliance with a higher alien power. The same, almost feudal, hierarchy of management exists here: at the bottom are the silent Devil's End villagers and Garvin the verger, the equivalent roles to the prisoners turned prison-guards in *The Mind of Evil*. On the next rung up are the villagers with dialogue – Bert the Landlord and Squire Winstanley – whilst on the top are the series regulars and Miss Hawthorne. The important thing to note in this context is how the middle-ranking figures, the pub owner and the local gentry, are in a similar Faustian role (albeit encouraged through hypnotic control) to that of the Master and the alien power.

The idea of layers of authority is important in Pertwee stories, both before and after *The Dæmons*, particularly those written by Robert Sloman. Consider *The Green Death* and *Planet of the Spiders*. In the former story, the role that would have been the Master is taken by Stevens, the boss of a chemical company who controls his workforce through brainwashing, but is himself under the control of a supercomputer called (ominously for Stevens) BOSS. In *Planet of the Spiders*, the antagonist is Lupton, a retired businessman who retreats to a mediation centre and, in a quest for knowledge, begins to exert his influence on his fellow guests, but soon finds himself controlled by more powerful forces. In short, Sloman seems preoccupied by the ways humans, particularly businessmen, find themselves in a power struggle with an alien entity that ultimately turns them into a crushed middle manager, and *The Dæmons* represents this on a variety of levels that include the Master and the villagers.

Surprisingly, in Haynes' terms, Pertwee's Doctor can also be seen as a Faustian character. From his first story, *Spearhead from Space* (1970), he is presented as 'a Promethean figure who asserts the rights of man over a tyrannical order that seeks to enslave him'[49]. The starting point for this is the trial of the second Doctor in *The War Games*. The Doctor has been accused by the Time Lords of interfering in the affairs of other races, and, found guilty, he is exiled to Earth with his knowledge of how to operate the TARDIS removed. The underlying stories that thread through the Pertwee years are the Doctor's attempts to regain this knowledge, the science he employs to try to bypass the Time Lords' punishment and the Time Lord missions he is forced to undertake. In his quest for knowledge the Doctor allies with the Time Lords (who are able to grant him freedom) and, Prometheus-like, with UNIT (in return for access to a laboratory). In Renaissance terms, the Doctor preoccupies himself, like Faust, with a combination of 'classical learning' with his tinkering with technology, and 'magical science' with his quest for the secrets of time travel.

The third Doctor, above all others, is shown to be a character who is obsessed with the acquisition of knowledge, whose conformity acts as a carapace to hide his true maverick independence. For all his Earth-bound quirks (his pomposity, his London clubs, his political acquaintances and his friendship with the Brigadier), he is a man who is desperate to leave the Earth and return to being (to steal a phrase) a 'cosmic hobo'. As Inez Hedges states:

> 'the Faust story posits the new place of humanity in a world whose very foundations were being shaken by scientific discovery. Faust thirsts after knowledge above all else, because he believes it will unlock the key to the universe.'[50]

---

[49] Haynes, *From Faust to Strangelove*, p19.
[50] Hedges, *Framing Faust*, p5.

What's more, the Doctor is prepared to make a Faustian bargain with both Gallifrey and UNIT in order to return to his exploration, for him the 'key to the universe', and, by *Planet of the Spiders*, we see how this quest for knowledge leads to his downfall. In *The Dæmons*, however, his role is more conventional: that of a man trying to break a number of Faustian bargains in a way that causes the least amount of damage.

Sloman's stories are full of these Faustian bargains that play out in layers of characters who think they are in control, only to find a higher authority. What makes *The Dæmons* distinctive in this is the way it boils this down to the fundamentals of the Faust myth: a layering of authority that includes a bottom stratum consisting of the uninformed and silent (the villagers); a second order stratum consisting of human authority (Bert and Winstanley), blind to the nature of the control imposed upon them but controlled all the same; a third stratum consisting of the occult Faust-figure, a dissident conjurer who thinks he's in control until the final revelation (the Master); and, finally, a top layer consisting of the entity who really is in control (Azal). With this clearly defined layering of characters, *The Dæmons* concludes the story of the Master through the season, emphasises in retrospect the position the Master has in the five stories and begins the theme of middle-management that runs through Sloman's stories and concludes with *Planet of the Spiders*.

This goes some way to explain *The Dæmons* in magical terms - on the other side of Clarke's 'third law' is advanced science. *The Dæmons*, and the stories surrounding it, play lightly with the Faust myth in its treatment of scientists. So far I've focused on how the story riffs on the character of the magician and occultist, but it is appropriate for a story that blurs science and magic to such an extent that it is important to also look carefully at the cultural role of the scientist. Fortunately, in this area someone has already done a lot of the legwork for me.

'Science, Miss Hawthorne'

In her book *From Faust to Strangelove*, cultural historian Roslynn Haynes explores the evolution of representations of scientists in Western literature from the alchemist 'driven to pursue an arcane intellectual goal that carries suggestions of ideological evil' to the scientist as idealist, 'a figure holding out the possibility of a scientifically sustained utopia.'[51] Malcolm Hulke, the man who wrote a number of Pertwee stories including scientist-heavy *The Silurians* and *Invasion of the Dinosaurs*, told script editor Terrance Dicks that the risk of exiling the Doctor to Earth would be a series of stories limited to those involving alien invasions and mad scientists[52]. This risk lead many of the writers of the Earthbound stories, including Hulke himself, to push their stories in different directions to avoid the predicted clichés. Far from being a limitation, the idea of a scientist as antagonist and hero is a rich and compelling one. *The Dæmons* is another demonstration of the versatility of the concept of the scientist.

There are three different scientists in *The Dæmons*, each aligning with one or more of Haynes' types: the Doctor, the Master and Azal the Dæmon.

The Doctor's role is clearly that of heroic scientist; indeed Haynes

---

[51] Haynes, *From Faust to Strangelove*, pp3-5.
[52] Wood, *About Time*, p46.

directly references the Doctor in her chapter, comparing him to characters from HG Wells' and Jules Verne's novels[53]. Haynes subdivides this archetype into different categories: the scientist as inventor, the scientist as detective/adventurer, the scientist as world saviour, and the scientist as Utopian ruler, mostly drawing on texts from the late 19th and early 20th centuries. It is clear that even in just *The Dæmons*, the Doctor can be seen to manifest the first three of these subcategories. He investigates the events at Devil's End, he designs and helps Sergeant Osgood (again a scientist, but unfortunately too small-fry to make the list above) to build an energy converter to break through the heat barrier, and finally he confronts Azal in order to save the Earth. Through the story the Doctor is a combination detective, inventor and saviour – paralleling, according to Haynes, the roles of Sherlock Holmes, Thomas Edison and Abraham van Helsing[54]. The one category the Doctor doesn't inhabit is that of the Utopian ruler; indeed, it is this role that the Doctor so vehemently resists at the end of the final episode when Azal offers to grant him power instead of the Master. These roles are an excellent summation of the Doctor, and his reluctance to accept power, even for the purposes of good, is a defining attribute of the role, and one that separates him from the villainous scientists in the series.

As we have seen, the Master is the central Faustian character in *The Dæmons*, using occult science to summon Azal and to control the villagers. The Master falls, in Haynes' terms, into the category of the evil alchemist. His role as a scientist is drawn from the pre-Enlightenment, when science was, intentionally, mysterious and

---

[53] Haynes, *From Faust to Strangelove*, p167.
[54] Haynes, *From Faust to Strangelove*, pp169-78.

impenetrable to the outsider – see, for example, how the Master uses unintelligible words muttered under his breath to control the elements or Bok, Azal's gargoyle acolyte. Haynes notes that at the centre of the alchemical tradition were 'processes that ordinary people cannot understand' and that the incantations and symbols 'represent an almost insuperable barrier to non-scientists wishing to understand it'.

Compare this with the Doctor's approach to science through the story. The Doctor is constantly offering (occasionally delayed) explanations for what is happening. Indeed, scenes in which the Doctor tries to demythologise science dominate the third and fourth episodes as he gives a presentation about the Dæmons to his companions within the village, and a seminar on electronics to Osgood and the Brigadier outside the heat-barrier. The Doctor is always explaining science, whilst the Master relies on the mystery of ancient and alien science to maintain power.

Between these two opposing depictions of scientists is Azal. The Dæmon, as the Doctor points out, is not a god, but is an individual member of a race of powerful but amoral scientists who conduct experiments on other planets. Haynes (naturally) has a category for this:

> 'Of all the charges against the scientist in literature, none has been levelled more frequently or more vigorously than that of aloofness and emotional deficiency.'[55]

Haynes places the 'amoral scientist' as a subset of the 'impersonal scientist', a characterisation she supports with three main

---

[55] Haynes, *From Faust to Strangelove*, p211.

illustrations, all of which has an impact on how we view Azal: robots, human guinea-pigs and bomb-makers[56]. In short, the amoral scientist approaches the experiment with a dispassionate but logical focus. Unlike the heroic scientists they are not aiming to benefit mankind, and unlike the alchemists, they are not aiming for personal power. Instead, they are effectively robots, experimenting to advance science regardless of the effect on the subjects they are experimenting on. They think nothing of using humanity and human individuals as sources of material for research. Azal is willing, like the bomb-making scientists of the 20th century, to contemplate the destruction of the world. Despite being a character who is on screen for a short time, Azal has all these attributes and more. Indeed, the fate of Azal almost over-emphasises his computer-like amorality: when Jo places herself between Azal and the Doctor at the climax of the story, the Dæmon struggles to understand the logic of her action and, in the words of the Doctor, blows 'a fuse'. By the end of the story, Azal is so much the impersonal scientist that he becomes as much a robot or computer as BOSS, the electronic antagonist in *The Green Death*, driven by logic and defeated by human irrationality.

These three types of scientist, so neatly defined through the three characters in *The Dæmons*, are telling as they are drawn from different times in the evolution of science. The Master is a Faustian alchemist employing apparently archaic rituals that turn out to be an alien form of obscure and occult science. The category of scientist the Doctor falls into is, appropriately given the character's original literary influences, a blend of the Victorian and Edwardian using science as a way of improving, detecting and exploring the

---

[56] Haynes, *From Faust to Strangelove*, pp241-263.

world. Finally, Azal's form of science comes, unexpectedly, from the 20th century, a combination of J Robert Oppenheimer (physicist and 'father of the atomic bomb') and Josef Mengele (infamous doctor at Auschwitz, the 'angel of death'). There is a circularity with the science in the story: the Master uses science so ancient that it looks like magic to summon an alien whose science is closer in morality to our own, and in the middle lies the Doctor: an idealist and rationalist, but above all a humanist.

Tying these different sciences together and creating a bridge between the knowledge-hungry Faustian alchemy of the Master, as character who fetishises control and domination, and the amoral, dispassionate and apocalyptic science of Azal, is politics. And this is where Aleister Crowley and Dennis Wheatley enter the story.

Prince of the Thriller and the Wickedest Man in the World

Historian Elliot Rose described Aleister Crowley variously as a 'dilettante diabolist' and as a 'would-be necromancer'[57]. In the 1910s and 1920s, Crowley allegedly spent a considerable amount of time and money attempting to summon the Devil. According to the thriller writer Dennis Wheatley, Crowley's mission to invoke Pan during the 1920s drove him ever more insane and made him spiritually impotent[58].

Born in October 1875, the child of members of the Plymouth Brethren, Crowley was a poet, mountaineer and novelist. Possibly as a rebellion against his strictly religious background, when he

---

[57] Rose, Elliot, *A Razor for a Goat*, pp50, 150.
[58] Hutton, *The Triumph of the Moon*, p262.

went up to Cambridge he became involved with libertarian societies. If he had been 20 years older he might have followed the decadent path of Oscar Wilde; if he had been 20 years younger and more inclined to the political left, he might have been tempted by the life of a spy like Guy Burgess, Donald Maclean, Kim Philby or Anthony Blunt. Instead Crowley became involved in the elite underworld of esoteric organisations similar to Freemasonry such as the Hermetic Order of the Golden Dawn and the Ordo Templi Orientis, which he ultimately led and shaped in his own philosophical image[59].

The life of Crowley is difficult to summarise, partially because of the sheer number of stories about him and the number of creative people he engaged with, but also partially because of the questionable veracity of those stories. Crowley was a self-promoter who surrounded himself with other self-promoters, each with their own motivations and reasons for developing rumours about him. He may have been, as Wheatley suggests, a committed but misguided searcher for power through magic who burnt himself out, but alternatively he might just have been a hedonist who frittered away any money he earned, on parties and, in the middle of his life, a robust heroin addiction. The truth of Crowley's life is difficult to pin down, but in a sense this isn't really an issue. There are two Aleister Crowleys: firstly the myth constructed by the anecdotes and by versions of him in books and later on film, and secondly the man, slowly withering under the weight of his notoriety and under his own predilection for pleasure.

One person responsible for bringing the myth of Crowley to the

---

[59] Hutchinson, Roger *Aleister Crowley: The Beast Demystified*.

forefront of the public imagination was Dennis Wheatley. Wheatley was born in January 1897, 22 years after Crowley. He was a delicate child and, like many such children in the Victorian and Edwardian years, it was thought best to send him to a series of tough, remote and character-hardening public schools[60]. Unlike Crowley, Wheatley did not succeed academically and instead travelled Europe, fought in France during the First World War and then finally took over the family business. His life took a different path after the Great Depression when his business collapsed and Wheatley decided to turn to writing.

At first, his books were fairly straightforward action thrillers anticipating the **James Bond** books of Ian Fleming (an author whose life and personality closely mirrored Wheatley's), but by the mid-1930s, following a poor review of his latest book, *The Fabulous Valley*, he was encouraged to inject something different into his favoured genre[61]. In the early 1930s, Wheatley began to research the world of black magic and was introduced to a now ailing and penniless Crowley. Crowley bequeathed a signed copy of his *Magick in Theory and Practice* to Wheatley for his collection and research for which Wheatley was grateful. Then Wheatley met a man who shared his and Crowley's beliefs but who proclaimed himself to be an enemy of the occult: alleged Satanist turned unlikely priest, Montague Summers (1880-1948).

Like Crowley, Summers, was attracted to the occult whilst at university and engaged in Black Masses until he received what Phil Baker describes as a 'violent spiritual shock' and turned, instead,

---

[60] Baker, Phil, *The Devil is a Gentleman*, pp49-54
[61] Baker, *The Devil is a Gentleman*, p295.

towards God[62]. He became a priest, or at least claimed to be a priest – there is some doubt about whether he was ordained and, indeed, the Catholic Church did not approve of him. Summers became the model for the anti-Satanist, witchcraft-hunting heroes of Wheatley's fantasy novels, connecting Margaret Murray's beliefs that witchcraft was a religion with a lineage unbroken since ancient Egypt with accusations of devil worship and diabolical power. He was an historian of the occult, but one whose fervent belief in the subject compromised his objectivity. Like Crowley and Gerald Gardner he was a man who understood the low cultural appeal of the occult to the general public and was able to align it with the elite and impenetrable world of strict Catholicism. High and low culture together again.

The influence of Crowley and Wheatley continues to cast a shadow today. For example, the third book in Stephen Volk's trilogy of novels featuring key figures in the occult and horror (the first two telling stories based on the lives of Peter Cushing and Alfred Hitchcock) focuses on the relationship between the occultist and the thriller writer[63].

Crowley and Summers became the twin poles of Wheatley's occult research, and the founding influences on his first work of fiction, and key influence on *The Dæmons*, *The Devil Rides Out*. However, beyond the occult trappings of Wheatley's novel, there are other elements that connect the lives of Crowley and Wheatley and his books to **Doctor Who** in the early 1970s, namely the connections between the occult and politics.

---

[62] Baker, *The Devil is a Gentleman*, p312.
[63] Volk, Stephen, *Netherwood*.

'Leafing through the French Fascist paper, *Gringoire*, George Orwell noticed no less than thirty eight advertisements for clairvoyants. He remembered this when he was trying to fathom the relationship between occultism and right wing politics. For one thing, occultism replaces the idea of progress and the untidy reality of change with a timeless and reassuring vision of eternal myth, instead of real history, as if nothing essential had changed since the days of ancient Egypt. Secondly, occultism and Fascism share a sense of spurious elitism, esoteric knowledge being the dominion of a special few and the guarantee of their superiority. More than that, occultism offers a transcendence of ordinary life, and an idealist fantasy of pure mental power without normal economic or social restraints.'

[Phil Baker][64]

As Orwell outlines, there is a heritage and a sense of exclusivity to both far right wing politics and the occult that attracts followers of the former to the traditions of the latter. Historian Ronald Hutton suggests that throughout his novels, Wheatley 'expressed the viewpoint of a traditional British political conservative'[65], whilst Baker describes both Wheatley and Crowley as 'high Tories', suggesting that they 'both liked good food and drink, they were both rather Edwardian [...] and in later life they were both proud of their resemblance to Churchill.'[66] There is, therefore, a deeply political subtext to the occult, particularly as interpreted by Wheatley. Hutton goes on to suggest that 'Wheatley's portrait of

---

[64] Baker, *The Devil is a Gentleman*, p303-4.
[65] Hutton, *The Triumph of the Moon*, p264.
[66] Baker, *The Devil is a Gentleman*, p299.

Satanism was of a highly organised international conspiracy to subvert the "Western" world'[67]. In the 1930s, this had a simple anti-foreigner slant, but by the time *The Dæmons* was made, this conspiratorial mode had taken on a different flavour.

There was a societal and cultural shift between the 1960 and 1970s in terms of who were perceived as enemies, and where the threat of societal collapse came from. In the 1960s this threat came from 'outside': from the Soviet Union in reality, and from aliens in science fiction. Popular culture in the 1960s focussed mainly on alien invasion and conquest as a mirror of the still recent memories of the Second World War and as a proxy for the less tangible, but no less frightening effect of the Cold War and the atomic bomb. In the 1970s, traces of this remained, but they were joined, and often replaced, by a new source of threat: from within. This mostly focused on America, but the effect of the shift, and the anxiety, spread to Britain and British culture. The anti-Vietnam and civil rights protests and the rise of the hippie counterculture, all contributed to a fear of authority and of institutions, ultimately leading to paranoid and surveillance thrillers such as *Klute* (1971) and *Play Misty for Me* (1971), films that, in the words of Martin Rubin:

> 'reflected the [1970s] tendency to turn the focus of political paranoia strongly inward, towards America's own fundamental institutions, rather than towards external threats (such as communism or gangsterism) to those institutions.'[68]

---

[67] Hutton, *The Triumph of the Moon*, p265.
[68] Ruben, Martin, *Thrillers*, p149.

This happens in **Doctor Who** as well. In fact, in many ways the series was ahead of the curve when it came to the adoption of the paranoid thriller genre tropes. The easiest way to illustrate this is by comparing the Hartnell and Troughton so called 'base-under-siege' stories, where the threat comes from **outside**, with Pertwee stories such as *The Ambassadors of Death* (1970), *Inferno* or *The Claws of Axos,* where the threat comes (either entirely or partially) from **inside**. Unlike the earlier stories where the internal threat comes from a corrupt soldier or politician, in *The Dæmons* this idea is reframed on a level that gets even deeper to the heart of the British establishment. In *The Dæmons*, the conspiracy narrative is focused on a corruption of the Anglican church and on the institutions and parochial customs of the Home Counties village. Before examining this, it is worth exploring how the political elements that tie the series to the right-wing libertarianism of Crowley and the paranoid conservatism of Wheatley also threaded through both the portrayal and the presentation of the third Doctor.

In an interview for Kevin Davies' anniversary documentary *Doctor Who: Thirty Years in the TARDIS* (1993), Verity Lambert, **Doctor Who**'s first producer, criticised the shift in the nature of the lead character between Troughton and Pertwee. She believed that by aligning the Doctor with UNIT and making him a 'scientific advisor', the anti-establishment roots of the Doctor were being compromised. For her, the Pertwee version of the Doctor somehow 'conformed' and lost some of his independence and rebelliousness. Paul Cornell riffed on this idea in his review of *Terror of the Autons* when it was released on video in 1993. He suggested that the third Doctor's name drops of civil servants and gentlemen's clubs through the story marked him as 'one of the bourgeoisie, a man at home with brandy and cigars', in short, Dennis Wheatley from Mars. Cornell summarises his case in the last sentence of the review: 'they exiled the Doctor to Earth to become a Tory.'[69]

Compared to the mercurial and anarchic Troughton, there is indeed something superficially conformist about Pertwee's Doctor. From the scenes in *Spearhead from Space*, we can see that, unlike his predecessor, the third Doctor is keen on getting his appearance correct: he takes time to choose clothes, tries on different hats and, finally, carefully selects his car. This focus on detail smacks of him trying to blend in, albeit in an ostentatious way, and, interestingly, might be seen as stemming from the approach to the part and the performance of Pertwee himself. Known as a comedian, Pertwee was keen to take the opportunity to break free of his typecasting as he indicated in an interview from 1975:

> 'Like Peter Sellers, I had always hidden myself under what's known in the theatrical business as a green umbrella. I'd always played character parts and eccentrics, I'd never allowed myself to be just myself [...] so eventually I just decided to play him as I felt, so really what the Doctor liked was just an extension of what I like.'[70]

So Pertwee based his performance on himself: a lover of modern technology and contemporary fashion and style. On the surface, therefore, the third Doctor is indeed more grounded in the modern world than his predecessors, and Cornell is correct that he appears

---

[69] Cornell, Paul 'Review of *Terror of the Autons*', *DreamWatch Bulletin* #112 (April 1993).
[70] Interviewed by John Hudson and Stuart Money in *Jon Pertwee Fan Club Newsletter* issue 3 (1975), cited in Howe and Walker, *The Third Doctor*, p18.

in his stories to be an embedded member of the establishment. Often this superficial conformism is routinely undercut with a mocking criticism; however, this is apparent particularly, though not exclusively, in the stories written by Sloman and Letts.

In the same way the Doctor's Faustian thirst for knowledge is developed and, ultimately, punctured by his fate in *Planet of the Spiders*, his high-Tory, Wheatley-esque affectations are also critiqued and undercut throughout the five seasons. Yes, the Pertwee Doctor is superficially pompous, materialistic and patronising, but, much like Troughton's apparent clownish ineptitude, these characteristics are frequently shown to be a front. The third Doctor works with authorities as a means to an end, and refers to his high-society contacts ('Tubby Rowlands', for example[71]) as a way of disconcerting his Earthbound adversaries. His pomposity is a source of humour, his claims to have the answer are frequently undercut by circumstances. In a sense, the Pertwee Doctor is as clownish as Troughton's, but he is shaped by his exile.

In *The Dæmons* this satirising of the right wing threads through almost everything in the story, but also shapes how it responds to the occult conspiracy narratives of Wheatley. *The Dæmons* is not a homage to Wheatley in the same way that *The Talons of Weng-Chiang* is a homage to Conan Doyle and Sax Rohmer. Instead, it takes explicit elements and themes from Wheatley's black magic thrillers and subverts them. I've already noted that the relationship between *The Dæmons,* science and magic is a complex one. The same is true with the way it intertwines the occult and politics. The devil, devil-worshipper and devil-worshipper-hunter characters are

---

[71] *Terror of the Autons* episode 3.

all not as they seem. It might be worth doing some comparisons between *The Dæmons* and *The Devil Rides Out* to get an idea of this.

Hunting the Devil

On the surface, *The Dæmons* looks like *The Devil Rides Out*: it draws on the same visual iconography, namely the Devil as the 'goat of Mendes' or 'Baphomet', a depiction of the Devil in animal form that has its source in the accusations made against the Templars in the 14th century[72]. In terms of characters, *The Dæmons* also superficially resembles *The Devil Rides Out*. Both include a Satanist as an antagonist and an anti-Satanist as a protagonist. This is not unusual for **Doctor Who**. The series is notorious for harvesting imagery and ideas from genres such as horror, thrillers and science fiction and integrating them into the format of the series. **Doctor Who** is, in essence, a text built like fan fiction, poaching from other texts, such as *The Devil Rides Out,* to create something more conceptual and ironic than the original[73].

This matching is complicated, however, by the idea of the Master and the Doctor (the Satanist and anti-Satanists in the story) as characters who are in disguise. The story moves beyond pastiche, playing upon the characters of the Master and of the Doctor, presenting both as a Matryoshka doll of character types: the Master as an alien disguised as a Satanist disguised as an Anglican vicar; the Doctor as an alien disguised as an eccentric human disguised as a member of the authoritarian elite. *The Dæmons*, with its melange

---

[72] Rose, *A Razor for a Goat*, p126.
[73] For those unaware of Wheatley's original story, see the Appendix for a summary of the plot of *The Devil Rides Out*.

of Faustian themes, occult popular culture and distillation of the scientist character, is perhaps the most pure version of the idea of the series as textual poacher.

In his study of the relationship between Satanism and witchcraft, *A Razor for a Goat*, Elliot Rose offers a useful taxonomy of devil worship, four schools of thought that distinguish between different views of what Satanism really was: the Bluff School, the Knowing School, the Anti-Sadducee School, and the Murrayite School[74]. The Bluff School denied everything, believed that witchcraft and Satanism didn't exist, and was characterised by common sense and scepticism. The Knowing School believed that witches worshipped the Devil, but, like the Bluff School, believed that the worship was without any power or effect. The Anti-Sadducee School was the polar opposite of the Bluff School, believing that not only did witches worship the Devil, but that this worship had a real and dangerous power. The Murrayite School, as the first chapter of this book should make clear, believed in witches and the Devil, but through pseudo-history and dodgy folklore represented the relationship between the two in the context of an ancient religion[75]. We have already seen which character falls naturally into the Murrayite School, but the other three Schools also offer an interesting set of comparisons to both *The Dæmons* and *The Devil Rides Out*.

The Duke de Richleau in *The Devil Rides Out* is clearly an anti-Sadducee. When he fights the Satanists he is fighting what he sees not as deluded acolytes of Mocata, but as followers of a real and

---

[74] Rose, *A Razor for a Goat*, pp8-9.
[75] Rose, *A Razor for a Goat*, pp8-14.

malevolent supernatural power. The Duke is the epitome of political authority both in a corporal sense, with his aristocratic title and attitude, and in a temporal sense with his Catholic spiritualism. The equivalent character to the Duke in *The Dæmons* is the Doctor, but the Doctor, far from being an anti-Sadducee, is clearly embedded in Rose's Bluff School, a rationalist and a modernist, but one that, tellingly, poses as a kind of hybrid of a Murrayite and anti-Sadducee throughout. His use of iron and a faux-spell to repel Bok, his remote control of Bessie, and his (reluctant) posing as the wizard Quiquaequod to fool the credulous villagers are all moments where the Doctor takes advantage of the appearance of magic to get out of a sticky situation. In short, the third Doctor does what he has always done: he uses the appearance of conformity (in this case Wheatley's ideal of spiritual authority) to mask his true, anti-authoritarian nature. The third Doctor is not a high-Tory anti-Sadducee like the Duke de Richleau, but he's not against letting his enemies think he is.

So what of the Master? Tellingly, the Master is both on the surface, and within his disguise as Magister, the opposite of the Doctor. As Magister, the Master is the Satanic power that an anti-Sadducee would fight against. In this battle, therefore, it would be Magister versus Quiquaequod, and indeed the story concludes with the Doctor using his 'magical' control of Bessie to capture the Master. So Magister is a clear recreation of Mocata – but Magister is just a front. The Master, far from being a real Satanist, is merely an alchemical scientist who recognises the power of incantations and rituals as part of an advanced science. In this way, seems to be in the Knowing School: he believes in the worship of the Devil, but does not believe that the power involved is a supernatural one.

Whilst the story does indeed draw heavily upon Wheatley, the real parallels lie only in the false layer that Magister and Quiquaequod operate on. Above this, the Master and the Doctor are fighting in the rational, modern world of the Bluff and Knowing Schools. This is a perfect representation of how the Doctor operates in *The Dæmons*, and it's not so far from how the third Doctor (particularly) behaves in general. The Master is known for his disguises, but the Doctor has always hidden his true intelligence and personality behind a mask, from the second Doctor's adoption of a childlike innocence all the way to the ninth Doctor hiding his post-Time War trauma behind humour. In the case of the third Doctor, this results in the appearance of a man of conventional authority, even elitism, concealing an anti-establishment heart. *The Dæmons* takes Wheatley's tale of Satanic conspiracy and **blurs** it, poaching the elements that both distil the atmosphere of the original and ties it best to the subversive eccentricity of the series itself.

Chapter 3:
A Tour of Devil's End

Twelve miles from Aldbourne, the village where *The Dæmons* was filmed, lies Silbury Hill, a prehistoric, man-made mound that rises almost 40 metres above the chalk downland. Between 1968 and 1970, Silbury Hill was the site of an archaeological dig that was filmed and transmitted on BBC Two, a series of programmes that directly inspired the opening episode of *The Dæmons* and the BBC3 filming of Professor Gilbert Horner's excavation of the Devil's Hump. Two miles from Silbury Hill is Avebury, smaller than Aldbourne, a village that nestles within a stone circle and was used as the location for the 1977 children's drama **Children of the Stones**. Silbury Hill, Avebury, West Kennet Long Barrow, Stonehenge, all within an hour's drive of Aldbourne, are markers in an ancient landscape that has fed British mythology, folklore, Earth mysteries and popular culture for centuries. A psychogeographer's wonderland, the pocket of England around Aldbourne is not only a site of vital historical importance, it's also a stone's throw from the M4, the motorway that connects London with Wales and that formed a corridor along which location scouts from the BBC would cruise.

There is something about the English village that made it an enticing location for particular genres of popular culture in the 1970s. But why should such a parochial and picturesque location become such a standard for horror and dark fantasy? In the previous chapter, I inferred that the writers of **Doctor Who** were, like fan creators, 'textual poachers'. In this chapter, I want to press this idea further by looking at how the series adapts the work of genre writers including John Wyndham and Nigel Kneale, MR James and HP Lovecraft to create a new, gestalt narrative. Through this, I want to explore how the English countryside and pastoral mythology has been adopted and reshaped by popular culture before, during and after the production of *The Dæmons*. In this way I will unpack what the English village brought as a location for this story and others in the 1970s and 1980s, and what Aldbourne in particular contributes to the character and popularity of *The Dæmons*. This will be a whistle-stop tour through subjects ranging from folk horror and pseudo-archaeology to psychogeography, hauntology and religion.

Villages of the Damned

Before tackling how *The Dæmons* engages with the ideas and themes of Wyndham, Kneale, James and Lovecraft, I'd like to spend some time exploring the village itself. *The Dæmons* is one of those stories in which the geography of the location and the fictional setting forms part of the narrative, a story that, both within and outside the fiction, is preoccupied by the village. To understand *The Dæmons*, it is necessary to understand what Aldbourne/Devil's End brings to the story.

The village, as presented onscreen, consists of a central green with a church to the back, a pub, the Cloven Hoof, to the right, a buttercross (a stone column often found on village greens) off-centre, and three sides of terraced cottages. Outside the village centre, to the left of the church and a way up a rise, is the Devil's Hump, a Bronze Age tumulus. The village is surrounded by a tangled, leafy network of lanes and open spaces. Neighbouring villages include Satanhall, Witchwood, Abbotsburn and Covenstone (appearing fleetingly on a signpost as the Doctor and Jo journey to Devil's End), names that suggest the area is rife with dark, occult folklore.

In the real world, Aldbourne extends well beyond the village green. The Cloven Hoof, in reality the Blue Boar, has competition from the Crown, which lies to the south of the green. The earthworks are there to the north, but there are four of them, not one. None of them, as far as the records show, mark the location of an alien spaceship; instead archaeologists have discovered a disparate collection of beads, pins, flint flakes and evidence of cremation[76]. As I know to my cost, the roads around the real Aldbourne are almost as tangled as those around Devil's End, but the local place names are more conventional and less diabolical – the village is easily found so long as your map is consulted in the correct orientation.

The village of Devil's End is a dramatic condensation of a real physical location; a village that takes geographical and atmospheric elements from an actual place but transforms them into a space tailored to the requirements of the story. This isn't unusual in television of the time. Villages, particularly in the Home Counties along the M4 corridor, were attractive filming locations owing to their proximity to London and, relative to the city, the fact that the space could be controlled. The low populations, even lower during the working day, meant that filming could be conducted with minimal interruption and, in the case of *The Dæmons*, local residents could even be involved in the process. *The Dæmons*, as

---

[76] Pugh, RB, and Elizabeth Crittall, eds, *A History of Wiltshire Volume 1*, p206.

always, is a special case. It goes beyond using the village as a geographical setting, but instead uses the traditions and archetypal characters of the village to generate an atmosphere unlike other stories.

Perhaps the easiest way to unpack this idea is by comparing *The Dæmons* with the 1984 **Doctor Who** story *The Awakening*. Written by Eric Pringle and directed by Michael Owen Morris, *The Awakening* was made at a time following the success of *The Five Doctors* and the 20th anniversary celebrations when the production team was self-consciously mining the history of the programme to maximise nostalgia. *The Awakening*, therefore, can be read as an attempt at a version of *The Dæmons* for the 1980s.

The Awakening is set in the village of Little Hodcombe. The residents are in the middle of an English Civil War re-enactment, a harmless pageant to celebrate the history of the community, but the psychic and historical disturbances of the re-enactment have awoken the Malus, an ancient alien power lying dormant under the church. The Malus both feeds off and amplifies the emotions of the villagers, turning the war games into something more disturbing and real. The story is, like its predecessor, set almost entirely in a village, within which science and the supernatural, in this case ghosts, are blurring together. The village is isolated (in *The Dæmons* by a heat barrier, in *The Awakening* by the will of the villagers). Like *The Dæmons*, the story concludes with the destruction of the church and the breaking of a malevolent power that has bewitched the villagers.

Whether or not the connection between the two stories is coincidental, there is something undeniably nostalgic about *The*

Awakening. This isn't limited to the series referencing itself however. Both stories use the traditions of the village (both mythic and municipal) to create a sense of time-travel without the TARDIS[77]. This is an important aspect of the Pertwee story – a period of the show when the series was about a Time Lord (a term first used in *The War Games*, the story immediately preceding Pertwee's debut) who is incapable of time travel. It is telling that during this period, references to the Doctor's travels in time, his home planet and his fellow time travellers (the Master and Omega) increased, as if to compensate for the neutering of his ability. As a part of this *The Dæmons*, like *The Awakening*, is imbued with a feeling of **pastness**, and the village setting is the key to this. In *The Dæmons*, the village is presented as an archaic set of buildings, an archaic set of characters and an archaic set of rituals all combining to give the feeling of time travel, a feeling so successful that there is a jarring incongruity about the appearance of both the remote-controlled Bessie and the UNIT helicopter. Likewise, in *The Awakening*, the past (even more explicitly) haunts the present: scenes of Civil War soldiers and agrarian ceremonies become the norm, whilst the contemporary trappings of the village, such as the telephone box, become as out-of-place as the Doctor's TARDIS. There is a name in postmodern philosophy for this juxtaposition: 'hauntology'.

In 1993 in his book *Specters of Marx,* Jacques Derrida outlined his theory of 'hauntology'. Critic Chris Hughes summarises this theory as: 'the idea that there is something from the past which is always

---

[77] Whilst the TARDIS does feature in *The Awakening*, other factors in the story such as the war re-enactment contribute to the sense of time travel.

present in the present; and, also, that this something is waiting for its return in the future to come.'[78] Derrida, as the title of his book suggests, posited the idea of Marx and Marxism as a 'ghost' from history, waiting to return, but expanded this metaphor to latch onto a millennial preoccupation, seen also in writings by postmodern critics such as Jean Baudrillard, with the 'end of history'. Derrida argues that the theory of hauntology means that there is 'no end of history, because there are always 'specters waiting to return – there is always an, as yet, unknown future to come'.

More recently, the meaning of the term has expanded to include a form of anti-nostalgia that presents the 'in-memoriam' past (for example the 1970s and 1980s) as a place of danger and darkness. But even considering the original sentiment of the idea, and taking (perhaps perversely) the roots of the theory in Marxism out of the equation, it is clear how this collision of nostalgia, history, politics and the supernatural can apply to both *The Awakening* and *The Dæmons*. Both are stories set at, or near to, the time they are broadcast, and both depict the past as a dangerous corruption and a threat to the stability of the present.

Hauntology, in short, is a useful compensation for the lack of time travel within the series – instead the writers dwell on the archaic pockets of contemporary England (picturesque locations, country houses, old fashioned bureaucrats etc.) to give a sense of pastness

---

[78] Derrida, Jacques, *Specters of Marx: The State of the Debt, the Work of Mourning and the New International*; Hughes, C, 'Dialogue Between Fukuyama's Account of the End of History and Derrida's Hauntology', *Journal of Philosophy: A Cross-Disciplinary Inquiry* #7 (2012)

invading the present. In *The Dæmons*, this is compounded by the occult and folkloric elements. *The Dæmons* is a story that uses hauntology but blends it with genre themes such as the buried horrors of Nigel Kneale and MR James and the cosy catastrophes of John Wyndham, to create a story that somehow distils the key tropes of each.

Witchfinders and Buried Horrors

The term 'Folk Horror' is a relatively recent one but, like 'hauntology', it has taken on a life of its own and a feeling that it has been around for far longer. Originally defined by Piers Haggard, the director of *The Blood on Satan's Claw* (1971), popularised by Mark Gatiss in his BBC documentary series **A History of Horror**, and then codified by Adam Scovell and Andy Paciorek in *Folk Horror Revival: Field Studies* (2015), the term has brought to the fore (in some cases exhumed), a rich lode of movies that seem to be interconnected.

The core trilogy of *Witchfinder General* (1968), *The Blood on Satan's Claw* and *The Wicker Man*, are certainly thematically similar and share an approach to presenting on screen a dark vision of rural Britain and the power of the hidden mythologies that lie buried under its fields and concealed in its isolated villages. There is a sense of paranoia within the narratives of these films, and in many ways, the construction of these movies feeds off the same political conspiracies that gave rise to the original witch crazes of the 16th and 17th centuries. For example, *The Wicker Man*, directed by Robin Hardy and produced two years after *The Dæmons*, has at its heart a similar paranoid mode that is also found in the American Red Scare movies of the 1950s or even the

Watergate conspiracy thrillers of the 1970s.

In a sense, the term 'folk horror' is a little misleading and potentially reductive. One reason for this is that the terms 'folk' and 'horror' are both conceptual. Horror is a broader genre formed from a tangle of subgenres which, by itself, doesn't really define a film. Horror movies can be defined and arranged by content, style, themes, subtexts, actors and even, in the case of Hammer, studio. So the active concept in the folk horror genre is 'folk', but again this is a slippery and unsatisfactory term. It suggests that these films should draw on folkloric sources for their stories, which is fine until the nature of folklore itself is questioned. In this way, *The Blair Witch Project* (1999) and even the *Friday the 13th* (1980–2009) and *A Nightmare on Elm Street* (1984–2010) movies could be classed as folk horror. They are certainly horror movies, and the plots in each draw 'hauntologically' on something mythic from the past returning to threaten the present.

The term also precludes a wider range of films and television that either wouldn't usually be classed as horror, such as *Straw Dogs* (1971) or *Penda's Fen* (1974), and those which wouldn't normally be classed as folkloric in the same sense as *The Wicker Man*, such as *Invasion of the Body Snatchers* (1956) or *Village of the Damned* (1960), but nevertheless seemed to have shared themes with Hardy's movie. An alternative way to consider 'folk horror' is as a genre that balances setting and custom (rurality, isolated villages, sparsely occupied islands, agrarian rituals) with the skewed, dark stylings and twisted politics of film noir; one that harnesses the romantic and nostalgic appeal of what we would now call 'hauntology' and combines it with a picturesque (or at times anti-picturesque) depiction of the countryside. This sensitivity to the way the history of the landscape and the lost past of the Dark Ages and before, is a key to understanding the genre. Consider this in the context of the rise of occult societies in the 19th and 20th centuries – particularly that of Wicca, the New Age, home-grown religion that, as I've demonstrated, has links with *The Dæmons*. Ronald Hutton notes that:

> 'The 19th century [saw] the growth of Masonic societies, and the emergence of such groups as the Order of Wood Craft Chivalry. These seem to have grown out of a general Victorian romance with the ancient pagan world, imagined as bucolic and picturesque [and] in part dependant on a nostalgic idealisation of the countryside, resulting from a growth of industrialisation and urban living, and contributed to the modified resurrection of pagan-based folk customs.'[79]

Hutton's observations recall the merger of low and high culture. He describes the adoption and usurpation of the earthy 'working class' pagan with the Victorian middle class obsession with the ancient and pre-Christian. There are hints of hauntology here in the broadest sense of the term: the proletarian pagan world shaping the bourgeoise and conservative 19th-century world, anticipating the decline of Christianity in the following century and the rise in an interest in psychogeography. By the time the 1970s arrived this resurgence of interest in the occult had met the counter-culture of the long 1960s headlong and created the perfect environment to shape the way particular films and television dramas such as *The Dæmons* depicted the landscapes and customs of rural Britain.

---

[79] Ronald Hutton cited in Kryzwinska, Tanya, *A Skin for Dancing In: Possession, Witchcraft and Voodoo in Film*, p75.

There is certainly a strong thread of DNA that connects *The Dæmons* with the later cycle of folk horror films in the 1970s. Adam Scovell describes the story as:

> 'a key text in general Folk Horror if only because it distils just about every aspect of English esoterica into a neat package [...] *The Dæmons* summarises the early 1970s obsession with all things Magick more than most of the obvious, visceral examples.'[80]

Scovell surveys the superficial imagery that ties the story to the genre, but Tanya Krzywinska, a film and digital games historian, offers a comprehensive analysis of how the British mythic rural landscape is translated into folk horror narratives. A number of core texts of the folk horror genre (notably *The Wicker Man*), and by implication *The Dæmons*:

> 'are set in contemporary verdant rural landscapes. In the majority of British-made occult films, the countryside is more than simply a pretty backdrop for the action, as it is linked to the evocation of pre-Christian agrarian religious practices [...] *The Wicker Man* use[s] [Margaret] Murray's idea that the customs and practices of witchcraft have persisted in small isolated rural communities.'[81]

For Krzywinska, therefore, it is the combination of the geography, psychogeography, mythology and the history of the countryside that is the key to understanding the genre. In basic terms, it is this hauntological idea of time travelling without actually going back in time, the idea of accessing a place that is trapped (dangerously) in

---

[80] Scovell, *Folk Horror Revival*, p194.
[81] Kryzwinska, *A Skin for Dancing In*, p78.

the past and becoming trapped there yourself that feeds the genre of folk horror. So it is Sergeant Howie, the contemporary copper in *The Wicker Man*, being stuck on the pagan Scottish island with his aeroplane sabotaged, or the Doctor and his companions trapped behind the heat shield in Devil's End and threatened by malevolent Morris dancers, that connects these texts to the genre. Morris men, a broken aircraft, a supernatural heat shield – all these are examples of **anti-technology** acting as a barrier.

The Dæmons doesn't stop here, however. Beyond the occult horror cycle of the 1970s, the story also picks up and manipulates ideas and themes from the novels and television series of Nigel Kneale and John Wyndham.

Nigel Kneale (1922-2006) was a screenwriter and specialised as a writer of television thrillers, often with a science fiction or horror edge. His original **Quatermass** serials, transmitted in three series between 1953 and 1959 followed the titular professor as he confronted alien menaces in London and the Home Counties. In many ways, throughout the early 1970s, **Doctor Who** can almost be seen as an attempt to remake the **Quatermass** serials. In season seven, *Spearhead from Space* closely recreates scenes from **Quatermass II** (1955), whilst *The Ambassadors of Death* similarly adopts imagery and plot from the original **The Quatermass Experiment** (1953). It is the third **Quatermass** serial, **Quatermass and the Pit** (1958-9, remade (like its predecessors) as a movie by Hammer productions in 1967) that has the greatest effect on *The Dæmons*, however. **Quatermass and the Pit** opens with the discovery of skeletons at a London building site. Digging deeper, scientists find a buried metal spaceship, and inside that, the desiccated remains of insect-like aliens. It is revealed that these ancient aliens crash-landed thousands of years ago and, in order to preserve their race, pushed the evolution of *Homo sapiens* down the path that led to modern man, leaving a residue of 'race memory' that over time turned into superstitions about horned devils. This, as Kim Newman, notes, follows in the footsteps of Arthur C Clarke's *Childhood's End* (1953), a novel that featured aliens who 'don't show themselves to modern human until they've established their trustworthiness because their appearance (horns, leathery batwings) has shaped our image of the Devil.'[82]

John Wyndham (1903-1969) was a novelist who, like Kneale, specialised in science fiction set in England in the capital or the Home Counties. Through the 1950s he wrote a number of popular novels including *The Day of the Triffids* (1951) and *The Midwich Cuckoos* (1957). As with Kneale, through the 1970s **Doctor Who** drew heavily from Wyndham both in terms of tone and details of plot. In *The Dæmons*, for example, the heat barrier is drawn directly from a similar device in *The Midwich Cuckoos*, filmed in 1960 as *Village of the Damned*. Wyndham's novel opens with a number of car accidents on the outskirts of the village of Midwich in the fictional county of Winshire. It turns out that a mysterious hemispherical barrier consisting of some form of gas has formed at the edges of the village with the church at its centre. This method of containing a Home Counties village is clearly an influence on Letts and Sloman, but the most interesting connection is the position of the church at the centre of this device. The alien incursions in both *The Midwich Cuckoos* and the earlier *The Day of the Triffids* strike at the heart of the British establishment, and this establishment is tied irrevocably to the church. As historian of

---

[82] Newman, *BFI Film Classics: Quatermass and the Pit*, p71.

religious and cultural studies Marcus Harmes notes in his article *Martians, Demons, Vampires and Vicars: The Church of England in Post-War Science Fiction*, 'imbricated with monarchy and parliament and with its status upheld by statute, the Church of England is the State Church.'[83] In these texts, and by association in *The Dæmons*, the church is not just a building, but a representation of British order. Science fiction novelist Brian Aldiss described Wyndham's style as a 'cosy catastrophe'[84], suggesting that his stories rely on a tension between the middle-class parochialism of the settings and the extremes of the horror inflicted on them. Harmes unpacks this idea:

> 'Wyndham's novel interprets the disaster by showing its impact on the life of people in the English Home Counties. This "catastrophist" writing is also "middle class", a comment often made of Wyndham as a criticism. However, the setting and the people involved in the disaster, especially the vicar, provide a useful way to understand disaster. As people with comfortable lives and with the most to lose from either natural or preternatural disaster, the middle class's engagement with menace and catastrophe is captivating.'[85]

In his article Harmes compares the work of Wyndham and Kneale, specifically **Quatermass and the Pit** and *The Day of the Triffids*, revealing how these key texts chart the declination of the Church of England and how the decay of the church is framed politically. His

---

[83] Harmes, Marcus 'Martians, Demons, Vampires and Vicars: The Church of England in Post-War Science Fiction', *The Journal of Religion and Popular Culture*, Volume 30 No 2 (Summer 2018).
[84] Aldiss, Brian and David Wingrove, *Trillion Year Spree*, p279.
[85] Harmes, 'Martians, Demons, Vampires and Vicars.

central thesis is that these texts (and he includes *The Dæmons*) use the incursion of science fiction threat as a way of shining a light on the fragility of the Church of England at the time, and that in these texts, the C of E represents a fundamental institution, essentially national order and cohesion. The connections between Kneale, Wyndham and *The Dæmons* are obvious: **Quatermass and the Pit** provides the foundation for the science fiction narrative of Sloman and Letts' script.

I would extend Harmes' thesis to include other genres, particularly horror/fantasy with *The Wicker Man*[86]. I would also suggest that, by tying this in with Krzywinska's psychogeographical ideas of how the ancient landscape and pastoral myths of England (and Scotland in the case of *The Wicker Man*) contribute to this commentary on the church, the full impact of *The Dæmons* can be revealed. It is only then that the social and geographical construction of Devil's End can make sense. The treatment of Christianity in **Quatermass and the Pit**, *The Day of the Triffids* and *The Wicker Man*, therefore, is an important factoring to understanding how *The Dæmons* is culturally and spiritually situated in the 1970s.

It is clear that the different genres adopted by Letts and Sloman connect *The Dæmons* with a number of themes and anxieties of the time, particularly concerning political paranoia, nostalgic nationalism and the decline of religion. It's a rich and complex collection of ideas, but presented in a typically simple and streamlined way.

---

[86] It's worth reiterating that *The Wicker Man* was produced a couple of years after *The Dæmons*. My contention is not, therefore, that the **Doctor Who** story was influenced by Hardy's film, or vice versa, but rather that each draws on similar social and political trends.

Comparing *The Dæmons* with the later *The Wicker Man* also suggests a pattern in how the village is represented. The fictional village location in many folk horror texts is constructed around a number of archetypical focus points: a church, a pagan site (stone circles, megaliths, maypoles, barrows), a manor house or centre of local government and a pub. The scale of *The Dæmons*, typically for such a financially constrained series, means Devil's End is restricted to only three main locations: the church (and cavern), the barrow and the pub.

The Church

The church of Devil's End is pivotal in terms of both the narrative and the heat barrier that isolates the village. The way the church and Anglicanism are presented in *The Dæmons* is telling. There is a conventional vicar of Devil's End, but he vanishes before the story begins. There is a church in Devil's End, but we never see inside the main body of it: we only gain access to the vestry and the cavern below. Marcus Harmes notes that in *The Dæmons*,

> 'It is not unreasonable to see in Devil's End, a village left without a church building because aliens blow it up, a comment on the realities of urban existence in many parts of 20th-century England, when churches were closed, converted to secular uses or demolished. More tellingly, the doctrines taught within the church building were suspect.'[87]

Harmes suggests that the destruction of the church at the climax of the story is a 'violation of the Church's sacrality' that broadly represents the decay of the Church of England at the time. There is

---

[87] Harmes, 'Martians, Demons, Vampires and Vicars'.

merit in this argument, and Krzywinska goes to great lengths to support it, although I would suggest the 'violation' of the Devil's End church takes place before the climax of the story. The blowing up of the church in *The Dæmons* has the same significance, though a lesser degree of visceral shock, as the climax to *The Wicker Man* in which the main protagonist is burned alive in a pagan ritual. Similarly, *The Dæmons* ends effectively with paganism triumphant as villagers dance in the shadow of the ruined church. As with *The Wicker Man* however, the climax is only the final moment in a gradual symbolic and physical dismantling of the church.

In the first episode of *The Dæmons*, it becomes rapidly clear that the Devil's End church is built on, literally, dodgy foundations. Alastair Fergus presents his report from inside the 'notorious cavern' below the church where 'pagan man performed his unspeakable rites'. Ironically, the BBC's decision to rename the church crypt a cavern and to avoid any mention of 'God' so as not to offend Christian viewers adds somewhat to the sense of sacrilege[88]. The church, the intended moral and spiritual centre of Devil's End, is built on what would in an American horror movie be a Native American burial ground, a site of ancient and supernatural forces. Far from being an established institution, the Devil's End church was, in effect, doomed from the time of its creation. The church in the story is defined by an absence of what you would expect. We never enter the body of the church; instead we see the vestry and, through a hidden entrance, the cavern below. The vicar, Canon Smallwood, has disappeared mysteriously before the story begins whilst the verger is seemingly possessed. Smallwood has

---

[88] Howe, David J, and Stephen James Walker, *Doctor Who: The Television Companion*, p212.

been usurped (presumably murdered) by Mr Magister, a man with a liquid approach to Christianity: a postmodern existentialist when taunting Miss Hawthorne, and a fascistic mesmerist when seeking to control the Squire[89]. As Harmes notes:

> 'clergy members are a counterpoise to the overtly modish and technological developments which science fiction privileges, their teaching on major aspects of life such as the origin and development of humanity confounded by modern science, including science of alien origin.'

In the context of *The Dæmons*, the Doctor is the character who promotes science over religion and superstition, but it is the Master who silences the church through his murder of Smallwood and his use of alien science to resurrect Azal.

There is a strong contemporary political significance to this as well, one which features a name that **Doctor Who** fans would recognise. Harmes notes that:

> 'The Church and its clergy are more than convenient targets for writers to narrate social decay or to offer striking illustrations of the impact of alien intervention on Earth. Rather the science fiction narratives involving the Church of England have used this institution as a potent signifier of social and religious uncertainty.'

---

[89] In his **Black Archive** monograph focusing on *The Time Warrior*, Matthew Kilburn describes the Master in *The Dæmons* as theatrical, the character's costume as the Magister resembling that 'worn by Boris Karloff as Hjalmar Poelzig in the Universal horror film *The Black Cat* (1934)' (Kilburn, Matthew, *The Black Archive #24: The Time Warrior*, p50).

He then connects this 'religious uncertainty' to conservative campaigner Mary Whitehouse's decrying of the eroding morality in society and culture. Whitehouse, in Harmes words, 'even went so far as to suggest that the Church itself was contributing to permissiveness and social decay.'[90] Perversely, given the campaigner's antagonistic history with **Doctor Who** through the 1970s, in Devil's End Whitehouse's attitude is represented by one of the heroes: Miss Hawthorne. Hawthorne defends the status quo of the village, becoming the voice of the established church, silenced by the removal of Canon Smallwood by the Master. The third Doctor is a complex layering of anti-authority and middle/upper-class bureaucratic fetishist, a character who adopts the appearance of the political right wing in order to subvert and inveigle the establishment and to speak truth to power. This is **Doctor Who** turned inside out. Letts and Sloman use their depiction of religion in Devil's End to simultaneously critique and empathise with the conservative concerns of the time. But the setting of the Church in the fictional village has even deeper implications, one that leads, like Miss Hawthorne's dual role as religious advocate and agitator, to a reconciliation between the pagan and Christian.

In Devil's End, there is an absence of the routine you would expect in a village religious community: the services that take place, the black masses, are sporadic and take place below rather than within the church. In Wyndham's 'cosy catastrophes', routine and the effect of a corruptive alien influence on them are important. Harmes notes that:

> 'the origin, nature and meaning of these threats were what

---

[90] Harmes, 'Martians, Demons, Vampires and Vicars'.

Wyndham himself called "logical fantasy" meaning that he intended to extrapolate the impact of catastrophe on situations that were recognisably based on English daily routine rather than being set in outer space.'[91]

The myth of the English village is a community built around these routines and customs. We can see evidence of these in Devil's End as well as a corruption of them, from the black masses to the interrupted patrol of the local policeman. To compensate for these, the older customs, the May Day festivities, take over but, as in *The Wicker Man*, they now have a far more sinister and violent connotations. The Morris dancers are now aggressive and the maypole, a traditional symbol of birth and fertility, has become a signifier of death: a stake waiting for a sacrificial burning. Devil's End is a village caught between the pre-Christian rituals of paganism and the futuristic alien science of the Master and the Doctor, and trapped in this pincer movement, the Christian core of the village withers and decays. In *The Wicker Man*, this is more direct, throughout the 1973 film, Kryzwinska sees:

> 'prominent destitute carcasses of churches, akin to the remnants of the Stone or Bronze Age past that are part of the British rural landscape (such as barrows, chalk hill carvings and standing stones).'[92]

In their decaying form, the churches in the film have already begun to resemble pagan monuments, and Kryzwinska describes this as the aftermath of a battle between the opposing religions, with paganism coming out on top before the film even begins. The

[91] Harmes, 'Martians, Demons, Vampires and Vicars'.
[92] Kryzwinska, *A Skin for Dancing In*, p86.

suggestion is that in *The Dæmons*, we are instead witness to the battle itself, the moment when the church comes up against paganism. The reality of what is presented onscreen in *The Dæmons* is more complex, however. Far from being a battle between Christianity and paganism, the story presents the two in **balance**.

The Barrow

There is a symmetry in the depiction of the church in *The Dæmons* and the depiction of the Devil's Hump. In episode 1, both are inflicted with a desecration: the church by a black mass, the barrow by an invasive archaeological dig. In episode 5, both are blown up: the church notoriously on-screen, the barrow economically off-screen. Each location is given equal weight in both the story and physically in the village. Another quality that connects the barrow with the church is that of buried paganism which turns out to be something more complex, and chimes with the archaeological elements of the story.

A potent influence on the televised excavation of the Devil's Hump was the series of archaeological digs at Silbury Hill between 1968 and 1969. These digs were broadcast live for the **Chronicle** television series on BBC Two (1966-91) when archaeologist Richard Atkinson drove a horizontal tunnel into the 40-metre high chalk mound and cameras were there to record what he found. The findings were not as dramatic as its fictional counterpart: the Atkinson dig revealed some information about how the mound was constructed and, unfortunately, led to collapse of the hill[93].

---

[93] Watts-Plumpkin, Emma 'The Many Faces of Silbury Hill'.

The significant aspect of the Silbury dig was not the archaeology, however; it was instead the collision of the modern technology of television cameras with the ancient landscape and shovels and scrapers of the dig. Represented in *The Dæmons* in the tension between the modern Alastair Fergus and the down-to-earth Gilbert Horner, this juxtaposition is what **Doctor Who** does best. Jon Pertwee famously once stated that the fundamental appeal of the series could be summed up by the image of a Yeti sitting on a loo in Tooting Bec – the unnatural in the context of the natural – and this is just another iteration of this. In terms of archaeology this is perfect – the natural is the English countryside and village; the unnatural lies beneath. In *The Dæmons* there are touches of both MR James and HP Lovecraft.

Montague Rhodes James was an Edwardian antiquary who wrote a series of short ghost stories a number of which (notably 'Oh Whistle and I'll Come to You My Lad', 'The Treasure of Abbot Thomas' and 'A Warning to the Curious') featured buried objects imbued with curses that intellectually driven but misguided archaeologists and intellectuals dig up with dire consequences, in the words of Kim Newman, James' academics 'rush towards horrid fates when carried away by scholarly enthusiasm for delving into library catalogues or the Earth itself.'[94] James' stories had been adapted for television on a number of occasions prior and during production of *The Dæmons*.

Howard Phillips Lovecraft, born 30 years after MR James in 1890, was an American writer of weird and horrific fiction. His short stories often revolved around a mythic pantheon of alien gods who

---

[94] Newman, *Quatermass and the Pitt*, p63.

once ruled the Earth but then fell dormant, occasionally waking to wreak terror on the unsuspecting humans. Lovecraft's stories featured buried evil, both literally and figuratively. In his words (and note the archaic spelling of 'demoniacal'),

> 'Life is a hideous business, and from the background behind what we know of it peer daemoniacal hints of truth which make it sometimes a thousandfold more hideous.'[95]

This sense of corruption behind the surface of the earth takes on a new edge in a consideration of the occult nature of landscape, again something of particular interest when considering *The Dæmons*. Ronald Hutton, in his study of British occultism, states that:

> '[Lovecraft] took to an extreme degree that theme so common in Victorian and Edwardian high culture; that civilisation is a veneer over a morass of primeval horror and excitement. In Lovecraft's cosmology, the latter was represented by "the Old Ones", monstrous extra-terrestrial entities which ruled the world before and desired to do so again if they could attain entry points to it. Megalithic monuments and ancient pagan rites of human sacrifice were treated as aspects of the veneration of these beings, and witches were portrayed as their votaries, seeking to restore their rule.'[96]

In a letter to Emil Petaja in 1935, Lovecraft acknowledged James' influence on him, stating:

---

[95] Lovecraft, HP, *The H. P. Lovecraft Omnibus*, p65.
[96] Hutton, *The Triumph of the Moon*, pp253-4.

'The most valuable element in him – as a model – is his way of weaving a horror into the every-day fabric of life and history – having it grow naturally out of the myriad conditions of an ordinary environment.'[97]

James via Lovecraft, therefore, is an important source for Pertwee's toilet-bound Yeti, but Lovecraft takes James' stories of creepy buried malevolence one giant step further by introducing a pantheon of extra-dimensional gods to the equation. In his **Black Archive** examination of *Image of the Fendahl*, Simon Bucher-Jones thoroughly unpacks Lovecraft's fusion of Gothic and science fiction, but through his Jamesian influence, it is possible to see him as a shaper of fantastical historical as well as future fiction[98]. Lovecraft brought alien deities and buried them under the surface of small town America and behind the curtain of reserved society. *The Dæmons* translates this directly to rural England and English mythology, and taps into a similar collection of alien gods. *The* **Doctor Who** story combines the parochialism of James (with Horner and then the Doctor cast as the inquisitive academics disinterring terrors), with the cosmological themes of Lovecraft, (with the Doctor and the Master as translators for the alien gods). At the time *The Dæmons* was made, these themes had also entered popular culture through another route, that of Erich von Däniken.

Von Däniken was a pseudo-historian who posited the idea, and presented archaeological 'proof', that the Earth been visited by aliens throughout history and that these aliens (or 'ancient astronauts') had shaped the development of humanity. His theories

---

[97] H. P. Lovecraft to Emil Petaja, 6 March 1935.
[98] Bucher-Jones, *The Black Archive 5: Image of the Fendahl*, pp67-8.

connected archaeological sites such as the Egyptian and Mayan pyramids, the Nazca Lines in Peru, the Iron pillar of Delhi, the Easter Island statues and many other examples of art and architecture, framing them as evidence of alien intervention. This is archaeology at its most spurious and populist. The idea of buried history is intoxicatingly compelling, as the fiction of MR James or the **Indiana Jones** and **Lara Croft** movies testify. In reality the exercise of unearthing the past from under the soil is slow, disciplined and frequently revolves around shards of pot and fragments of bone. Von Däniken's ideas, as with Margaret Murray's theories on witchcraft, turbo-charged the subject by injecting it with the narrative structures of the conspiracy theory. In what Peter Hiscock described as 'undoubtedly the most persistent mythology about ancient humans to have emerged in the 20th century', Von Däniken's theories blended theology, archaeology and cosmology to create a version of history in which the truth of human development lies below our feet as well as above our heads[99].

Throughout the third Doctor's exile to Earth **Doctor Who** was riddled with versions of this idea, from the Silurians, the reptilian precursors of humanity forced into their underground bunkers by a cosmic catastrophe, to Omega, a Time Lord turned god, buried within a black hole. Even the nature of the Time Lords' punishment plays into this theme: the Doctor – a benevolent version of a Lovecraftian god – is trapped, effectively buried in the establishment of Britain, and the stories pull on the tension between his fondness for his buried state and his desire to return to the stars. Von Däniken's ideas have also been directly interpreted in

---

[99] Hiscock, Peter, 'Cinema, Supernatural Archaeology, and the Hidden Human Past' *Nuvem*. 59, 2012.

the series, notably in *Death to the Daleks* (1974), *Pyramids of Mars* (1975) and *Image of the Fendahl*. In *The Dæmons*, the setting of a Home Counties village and the two locations of church and barrow are telling. The locations also recall an 'Earth Mysteries' theory that directly reflects Von Däniken's approach to archaeology. Ronald Hutton described the 'ley-line' theory as:

> 'the belief that the surface of the planet was crossed by straight lines or corridors of energy, which had been recognised by ancient peoples and marked by them with a range of different monuments.'[100]

The idea was built around an observation by amateur archaeologist and antiquarian Alfred Watkins, in short that ancient features such as barrows and megaliths can be seen to be aligned in the landscape[101]. When Christianity arrived in Britain during the Anglo-Saxon era, churches were often built on pagan sites, presumably as an encouragement to the non-Christian locals to convert, so the Christian buildings then become part of Watkins' system of lines. The idea of a kind of paranormal energy flowing along these lines was a later addition in 1969 by esotericist John Michell in his books *The Flying Saucer Vision* and *The View Over Atlantis* in which, among other theories, he posited that the lines were, in fact, created to guide Von Däniken-esque alien spacecraft in to land[102].

This connection between the church and the barrow is literalised in *The Dæmons* when Sergeant Benton and Captain Yates track Azal's

---

[100] Hutton, *The Triumph of the Moon*, p364.
[101] Watkins, Alfred, *The Old Straight Track*.
[102] Michell, John, *The Flying Saucer Vision: the Holy Grail Restored* and *The View Over Atlantis*.

footprints over the fields, or the assessment of the size and shape of the heat barrier. These measurements are taken from the air in a way that is reminiscent of discovery of crop circles and features like the Nazca Lines. In this way, Benton and Yates and the others gain a god-like (or alien) perspective on the landscape, something that the ancient pagan could never achieve. In Kryzwinska's words ley lines represent 'buried indigenous paganism that has left its traces in rural life,' ones that can only be seen from the air[103].

The connection between the church and barrow is both a physical and symbolic one. The cavern below the church points to this idea: the church is built on pagan foundations whilst the barrow is built on alien foundations; the former houses Bok, Azal's acolyte, the latter Azal himself. In short, in the cycle of Von Däniken-themed **Doctor Who** stories, *The Dæmons* offers one of the most complete interrogations of these 'Earth Mystery' theories, with its complex layering of Pagan, Christian and alien locations with characters and themes from Lovecraft and James' buried horrors.

The Pub and the Final Pint

So the church and barrow are twin poles of the village, representing an axis formed of a collision of the pagan, Anglican and alien elements. The third main location in the story, and one that completes the construction of Devil's End ,is the pub.

The village pub is another site of what Marcus Harmes describes as 'English daily routine'. In the past it was the main social venue of the village and a location of business trading; more recently it's become a place to eat, drink and watch sport. On a secular level,

---

[103] Kryzwinska, *A Skin for Dancing In*, p80.

the trip to have an evening pint of beer has the same resonance and rhythm as attending communion, whilst the building itself, like a church, has a feeling of sanctuary. This is best summed up in the 2004 comedy movie *Shaun of the Dead* in which the pub becomes the last refuge of the zombie-besieged characters or in Edgar Wright's later movie, 2013's *The World's End* when the security of the English pub is dissected and then subverted. The pub, therefore, has come to represent ritual and sanctuary in the village and in popular culture just as the church has gradually lost those roles. In *The Dæmons* the meaning of the pub and the way it is used by the characters is complicated.

There is a feeling of secular refuge about the Cloven Hoof. It stands apart from the church and barrow, lacking the dark and gothic trappings of the former and the wild, elemental nature of the latter. This sense of refuge is apparent from the beginning when a man dies in the churchyard after leaving the cosy security of the inn. The Cloven Hoof is the first place the Doctor and Jo visit when looking for the barrow – a scene in which the cliché of a pub being populated by local people who fear or ridicule outsiders is played upon but ultimately dismissed. Even in this scene, the pub's secular nature is reinforced. The way the occult is described in the Cloven Hoof offers a viewpoint that is distinct from the reverence of the Master's acolytes and Miss Hawthorne and the rational dissection of the Doctor. Instead, the villagers treat the stories of 'queer goings on' with humour. Bert the landlord (at this point representative of the inherited, practical wisdom of rural England and not the Master's chief spy and disciple) suggests that he could offer the Devil a room in the pub in return for the notoriety the stories have brought the village.

After this, the pub becomes the centre of rationality in the story. It is the place the characters escape to that seems to be somehow protected from the Master (the character never launches an attack on the pub or physically enters it himself that we see). It is the place where Dr Reeves (the human rational voice in the story) examines both the Doctor and Jo, and where the Doctor delivers his lecture on the history of the horned figure. In short, the pub is the place in the story where the heroic characters can rest and a space where the writers can explain the plot to the audience. Whilst the landlord and many of his customers turn out to be Satanists, this conversion happens away from the pub, and once it has happened the only antagonistic characters to enter the Cloven Hoof are Bert and (before being quickly rendered unconscious by Miss Hawthorne's reticule) a malevolent Morris dancer.

The conclusion of *The Dæmons* finds the Master arrested and symbolically paraded around the green whilst the real villagers of Aldbourne cheer and boo. The church, minutes beforehand, has been destroyed, but this is curiously swiftly forgotten about and our heroes elect instead to celebrate May Day without the corruption of Azal and the renegade Time Lord. Real Morris men return to the green and, dragged by the more open Jo, a reluctant Doctor joins in the dancing. The Brigadier and Mike Yates consider joining them but elect instead to return to the sanctuary of the pub for their version of the sacrament, a pint. The final shot is a slow pull back showing the village green, the pub and the dancers, ironically filmed from the top of the church that had just been obliterated. Order is restored: the pub is once more central to the action, the church central to the way we view the village, the barrow has been destroyed off-screen and forgotten.

The moment also points to the future – to the way in which *The Dæmons* has evolved since it was transmitted. The fusion of the real and fictional villages with the real villagers booing/cheering the Master/Delgado and Nicholas Courtney's ad-lib of 'I'd rather have a pint' nods to two reasons for the enduring appeal to the story: *The Dæmons* as a source of convention anecdote, and the nature of the timeless location of Aldbourne.

Conclusion: *The Dæmons* through Time and Space

In the preceding chapters, I've tried to position *The Dæmons* in an historical and cultural context, using the story as a way of exploring the occult fringes of society, literature and film. The plot of *The Dæmons* is a simple one, playing on basic and elemental themes and stock characters, but when seen in the context of both the history of occultism and the culture of horror and science fiction fantasy, a little bit of digging uncovers a rich seam of conflicts and connections: science versus magic; past versus present; high versus low culture; the popular versus the exclusive.

For all the polar reactions to it over time, *The Dæmons* is an important **Doctor Who** story today – but not because it is representative of the series. It is not a model 'base-under-siege' story or a Hammer horror pastiche, and whilst it borrows from Nigel Kneale like earlier Pertwee stories, aside from the opening scenes it does not feature military or scientific institutions, labs or bases. It doesn't even feature the TARDIS or time travel. Somehow, despite all this it has become a reference point for a particular era.

The preternatural source material for the story gives *The Dæmons* a feeling of folkloric pastness whilst embedding it in firmly in the 1970s preoccupation with the New Age, but the magical transformation of the story from occult oddity to nostalgic touchstone is driven by something that lies beyond what we see on screen. There is a synergy, between the past/present nature of the transformations of *The Dæmons* and the sense of place the location of Aldbourne gives this story. Perhaps uniquely in the series' history, the filming of the story, the story itself and the subsequent memorialisation of the story in sequels and documentaries, have merged to produce a new text that transcends that of the five episodes. In short, *The Dæmons* isn't just the story of the accidental awakening of an alien god on the outskirts of a Home Counties village, it's become more than this. *The Dæmons* also tells the story of the rise of a new form of occultism and a new religion and the decline of Christianity. It tells the story of how fandom's perception of the 1970s has shifted and then shifted back and how nostalgia works in the world of **Doctor Who**.

From 1971 to the present day, *The Dæmons* has moved through time, its meaning shifting and adapting to the contemporary world. The relationship between the story and the history and culture of the occult has powered this journey, giving the story a strange mixture of the traditional and the atypical. Complementing this transformation of the story over the decades is the sense of place that the location filming lends the story. The village of Aldbourne gives *The Dæmons* a foundation, a feeling of solidity and timelessness that has connected with myself personally.

I first visited Aldbourne in 1995, the year I learned to drive. Visiting **Doctor Who** locations wasn't an obsession, but it was a way of exploring the area around where I lived, practising driving and generally spreading my wings. I grew up in Hampshire, half an hour south of the M4 corridor, a prime area for **Doctor Who** filming. Trips to these sites were adventures that coincided with a new found freedom in my life. They were expansions of my world as I explored, in ever increasing and ambitious distances, the landscape of my childhood. There was, and still is, a feeling of pilgrimage about these visits – of searching for and finding places which are, if not sacred, then significant to a fan of the series.

Aldbourne itself is a **Doctor Who** theme park. When I finally visited it, what I discovered was a remarkably placed series of locations from *The Dæmons*, all unchanged and all economically situated around the village green. Even the Devil's Hump, the barrow under which Azal slept, is only a half an hour's walk from the church, ironically closer than in the actual story. To paraphrase Alastair Fergus, Aldbourne has become part of the dark mythology of my own childhood. Exploring a location, particularly one like Aldbourne that is so unchanged, is an uncanny experience. These villages, sections of roads, woodland and beaches are like double exposures: solid, real and present, but at the same time under-laid with the fictional details of the stories. Arriving at these places is a combination of visiting them for the first time and, somehow, returning to them. It's like stepping inside the television, the landscape becomes a palimpsest with the nostalgia generated by the series scratched over by the act of moving from real location to location. In Aldbourne, the places of interest (church, churchyard, green, buttercross, pub and barrow) are still intact and recognisable.

Outside the pub in Aldbourne are two rubbish bins: one in the shape of a Police Box and the other in the shape of a Dalek. Ironically, it is the second pub in the village, The Crown, that now has the **Doctor Who** street furniture – a sign of how the series has integrated itself into the fabric of Aldbourne. The old village is unchanged since the filming: the church (apparently rebuilt after the death of Azal) still stands guard over the green and the buttercross and the pub. In the beer garden to the front of The Blue Boar is the pub sign from the story: a painting of a devil's cloven hoof planted in the earth – you occasionally see people having their picture taken with it. That's it for memorabilia aside from a few framed photographs inside the pub. Last time I was there they had been taken down, replaced by mementoes of the village's other claim to fame, as a base for American soldiers prior to D-Day in 1944. The pub passes through different owners, the cottages on the green are sold, bought and sold again, and the memories of the filming pass into legend, but, appropriately for a story that has a focus on ancient history and buried truths, the real memorabilia are not the bins or relics of the filming, but the fabric of the buildings and landscape itself.

Up at the four barrows, the grass grows. After all this time, there is no sign of the film crew, nothing left there to mark the presence of the BBC (either the BBC One or BBC3 crews). For non-fans, this area is one more in a plethora of sites marking the prehistory of the area, whilst the village is a pretty but anonymous example of the pastoral Home Counties – gentrified, elegant, perhaps a little stuffy and claustrophobic. For fans though, the barrows hold a more tangible significance; the path leading to them is imbued with a sense of crossing over, whilst the village is memorial, not only to a single story, but to an era of the series that has such nostalgic weight for those who made it and those who watched it.

The Dæmons, perhaps more than any other story, has woven itself into the mythology of the place at which it was filmed, but at the same time it has woven itself into the mythology of the series itself. Whilst there's a high quotient of nostalgia driving this, this is not the full picture. The instantly recognisable cluster of buildings around the green allow Aldbourne acts as a permanent monument to the story, but also the perfect, compact location for reunions and sequels. The occult theme of the story is constantly updating, flexible enough to reflect the evolving alternative subcultures and fantasy fiction as the years have passed.

In *The Dæmons* it is possible to see a blurring of reality and fiction. When Miss Hawthorne meets the four men in the village in the first episode, her liminality as a character is highlighted, but also, tellingly, it draws attention to the actress Damaris Hayman as one of the few female speaking parts in the story. Hayman and Hawthorne merge together through the story and through the creative transformations of the story in the years following the broadcast to the point where the actress gains a benign and revered witch-like status. This is not the only merging: when filming in the area there really were freak weather conditions that the production team had to mitigate for – Aldbourne and Devil's End merging; each gaining a kind of occult mythology. Finally this collision of reality and fiction reached a climax when the BBC received complaints over the destruction of a real church, some viewers unable to see where the mythology of the series ended and the reality of the production began.

Reality and fantasy; science and magic; space and time. *The Dæmons* is truly a story of paradoxes, conflicts, oppositions and collaborations. Over time these oppositions have given rise to new stories that continue the life of Devil's End with a refreshed, contemporary edge, but throughout all, the space of Aldbourne stands unchanging and seemingly eternal.

Appendix – *The Devil Rides Out*

Published in 1934, *The Devil Rides Out* by Dennis Wheatley is an occult thriller and the second of his novels (after *The Forbidden Territory* in 1933) to feature the Duke de Richleau.

Set in England in April and May 1935, the story follows de Richleau and Rex van Ryn as they fight to save the soul of their friend Simon Aron who has fallen under the influence of a black magician and defrocked priest called Damien Mocata. Mocata is seeking to gain control over the Four Horsemen of the Apocalypse by using the Talisman of Set and has lured Aron into his power with the temptation of using clairvoyance to play the stock market.

The story begins in London. De Richleau and Rex van Ryn meet for a reunion dinner but Aron fails to turn up. They race to Aron's house in St John's Wood only to find a Satanic party underway with Aron at its heart. They kidnap Aron and smuggle him to de Richleau's flat from where they plan their fight against Mocata's plan, first spoiling a Sabbat meeting on Salisbury Plain, then finally becoming besieged by demonic forces in the country home of another friend, Richard Eaton. The book ends with the defeat of Mocata through de Richleau's employment of the forces of light opposing his black magic.

As with *The Dæmons*, the book is distinguished by a combination of Home Counties normality with exotic occult activities. The book is constructed around the binary opposition between de Richleau and Mocata: both are foreign but the former is an aristocratic Anglophile monarchist who, we learn in later novels, occasionally worked for the British government. The latter, Mocata, is a French priest turned black magician, a combination of two real life acquaintances of Wheatley: Montague Summers and Aleister Crowley.

Whilst there are clear thematic and visual similarities between the two texts, unlike the battle between the rationality of the Doctor and the use of occult superstitions by the Master in *The Dæmons*, the contest between de Richleau and Mocata is a more straightforward one between dark and light magic, a kind of Christian/Occult hybrid and Satanism.

Bibliography

Books

Aldiss, Brian, *Billion Year Spree: The History of Science Fiction*. London, Doubleday, 1973. ISBN 9780297765554.

Aldiss, Brian and Wingrove, David, *Trillion Years Spree*. Thirsk, House of Stratus, 2001. ISBN 9780575039438.

Baker, Phil, *The Devil is a Gentleman*. Cambridge, Dedalus, 2009. ISBN 9781907650321.

Bucher-Jones, Simon, *The Black Archive 5: Image of the Fendahl*. Edinburgh, Obverse Books, 2016. ISBN 9781909031418.

Cornell, Paul, Martin Day and Keith Topping, *The Discontinuity Guide*. London, Virgin Publishing, 1995. ISBN 9780426204428.

von Däniken, Erich, *Chariots of the Gods: Unsolved Mysteries of the Past*. New York, Berkley Books, 1999. ISBN 9780425063859.

Derrida, J, *Specters of Marx: The State of the Debt, the Work of Mourning and the New International*. New York, Routledge, 1994. ISBN 9780415389570.

Frazer, James George, *The Golden Bough*. London, Macmillan and Co, 1890. ISBN 9781108047432.

Gibson, Marion, *Rediscovering Renaissance Witchcraft: Witches in Early Modernity and Modernity*. London, Routledge, 2018. ISBN 9781138025455.

Greenwood, Susan, *Magic, Witchcraft and the Otherworld*. Oxford, Berg, 2000. ISBN 9781859734506.

Haynes, Roslynn D, *From Faust to Strangelove: Representations of the Scientist in Western Literature*. Baltimore, Johns Hopkins UP, 1994. ISBN 9780801849831.

Hedges, Inez, *Framing Faust*. Carbondale, Southern Illinois UP, 2005. ISBN 9780809329038.

Heelas, Paul, *The New Age Movement*. Oxford, Blackwell, 1996. ISBN 9780631193326.

Heselton, Philip, *Witchfather: A Life of Gerald Gardner vol 2*. Loughborough, Thoth Publications, 2012. ISBN 9781870450799.

Howe, David J, and Walker, Stephen James, *Doctor Who The Handbook: The Third Doctor*. London, Virgin Publishing, 1996. ISBN 9780426204862.

Howe, David J, and Walker, Stephen James *Doctor Who: The Television Companion*. London, BBC Worldwide Ltd, 1998. ISBN 9780563405887.

Hutchinson, Roger, *Aleister Crowley: The Beast Demystified*. Edinburgh, Mainstream Publishing, 1999. ISBN 9781851589678.

Hunter, IQ, ed, *British Science Fiction Cinema*. London, Routledge, 1999. ISBN 9780415168687.

Hutton, Ronald, *The Triumph of the Moon*. Oxford, Oxford UP, 1999. ISBN 9780192854490.

James, MR, *Collected Ghost Stories*. Oxford: Oxford UP, 2013. ISBN 9780199674893

Jenkins, Henry, *Textual Poachers: Television Fans and Participatory Culture*. New York, Routledge, 1992. ISBN 9780415905725.

Kilburn, Matthew, *The Black Archive #24: The Time Warrior*. Edinburgh, Obverse Books, 2018.

Kryzwinska, Tanya, *A Skin for Dancing In: Possession, Witchcraft and Voodoo in Film*. Trowbridge, Flicks Books, 2000. ISBN 9781862360099.

Larner, Christina, *Enemies of God: The Witch-Hunt in Scotland*. London, Chatto and Windus, 1981. ISBN 9780859765183.

Lovecraft, HP, *The HP Lovecraft Omnibus*. London, Grafton, 1985. ASIN B0168SGAO2.

Macfarlane, Alan, *Witchcraft in Tudor and Stuart England*. London, Weidenfeld and Nicolson, 1970. ISBN 9780415196123.

Michell, John, *The Flying Saucer Vision: the Holy Grail Restored*. Abacus, London, 1967. ISBN 9780349123196.

Michell, John, *The View Over Atlantis*. Sago Press, London, 1969. ISBN 9780349123172.

Michelet, Jules, *La Sorcière*. Paris, E Dentu, 1862. ISBN 9781330047347.

Murray, Margaret, *The Witch Cult in Western Europe*. Oxford, Clarendon Press, 1921. ISBN 9781304099136.

Murray, Margaret, *Gods of the Witches*. London, Faber and Faber, 1933. ISBN 9781909735477.

Newman, Kim, *BFI Film Classics: Quatermass and the Pit*. London, Palgrave Macmillan, 2014. ISBN 9781844577910.

Pugh, RB, and Elizabeth Crittall, eds, *A History of Wiltshire Volume 1*, Oxford: Oxford UP, 1957. ASIN B0039VLVVO.

Purkiss, Diane, *The Witch in History*. London, Routledge, 1996. ISBN 9780415087629.

Ralley, Robert, *Magic: A Beginner's Guide*. Oxford, Oneworld Publications, 2010. ISBN 978-1851687138.

Rose, Elliot, *A Razor for a Goat*. Toronto, Toronto UP, 1989. ISBN 9780802067685.

Ruben, Martin, *Thrillers*. Cambridge, Cambridge UP, 1999. ISBN 9780521588393.

Scovell, Adam, ed, *Folk Horror Revival: Field Studies*. Print on Demand, Wyrd Harvest Press, 2015. ISBN 9781326376376.

Sloman, Robert, and Barry Letts, *Doctor Who The Scripts: The Dæmons*. London, Titan Books, 1992. ISBN 9781852863241.

Summers, Rev Montague, *The Discovery of Witches: A Study of Master Matthew Hopkins Commonly Call'd Witch Finder Generall*. London, The Cyame Press, 1928. ISBN 9781417976744.

Thomas, Keith, *Religion and the Decline of Magic*. London, Penguin, 1971. ISBN 9780140137446.

Trevor-Roper, Hugh, *The European Witch-craze of the Sixteenth and Seventeenth Centuries*. Michigan, Harper & Row, 1968. ISBN 9780140551341.

Volk, Stephen, *The Dark Masters Trilogy*. Hornsea, PS Publishing, 2018.

Volk, Stephen, 'Netherwood'.

Watkins, Alfred, *The Old Straight Track*. Abacus, London, 1974. ISBN 9781905315604.

Watt, Ian, *Myths of Modern Individualism: Faust, Don Quixote, Don Juan, Robinson Crusoe*. Cambridge, Cambridge UP, 1996. ISBN 9780521585644.

Wheatley, Dennis, *The Devil Rides Out*. London, Hutchinson, 1934. ASIN B00CJB9CVQ.

Wood, Tat, *Seasons 7-11: 1970-1974*. **About Time: The Unauthorised Guide to Doctor Who** #3. Revised ed, Illinois, Mad Norwegian Press, 2009. ISBN 9780975944677.

Wyndham, John, *The Day of the Triffids*. London, Michael Joseph, 1951. ISBN 9780141033006.

Wyndham, John, *The Midwich Cuckoos*. London, Michael Joseph, 1957. ISBN 9780141033013.

Articles

'Crucifixion without Blood', *Daily Mail*, 10 September 1968.

'Rector Faces Black Magic Inquiry', *The Times*, 24 February 1969.

Doctor Who: The Complete History

> Volume 17: *Colony in Space, The Dæmons* and *Day of the Daleks,* 20 April 2016.

DreamWatch Bulletin

> Cornell, Paul, 'Review of *Terror of the Autons*'. *DreamWatch Bulletin* #112, April 1993.

> Wood, Tat, 'Hai! Anxiety'. *Dreamwatch Bulletin* #115, July 1993.

The Guardian

'Man Died after Talk of Magic and Witchcraft'. 18 August 1970.

Harvey, Peter, 'Growth of Black Magic Cults Gravely Worrying Churches and the Police'. 6 April 1970.

Agar, Jon, 'What Happened in the 60s'. *British Journal for the History of Science* #41, 2008.

Harmes, Marcus, 'Martians, Demons, Vampires and Vicars: The Church of England in Post-War Science Fiction'. *The Journal of Religion and Popular Culture* vol 30 #2, Summer 2018.

Hiscock, Peter, 'Cinema, Supernatural Archaeology, and the Hidden Human Past'. *Nuvem,* #59, 2012.

Hughes, C, 'Dialogue Between Fukuyama's Account of the End of History and Derrida's Hauntology'. *Journal of Philosophy: A Cross-Disciplinary Inquiry* #7, 2012.

O'Brien, Steve, 'The Wilderness Years'. *DWM Special Edition* #50, August 2018.

Simpson, Jacqueline, 'Margaret Murray: Who Believed Her and Why?' *Folklore* #105, 1994.

Watts-Plumpkin, Emma, 'The many faces of Silbury Hill' *Current Archaeology* #293, 2014.

Films

Baker, Roy Ward, dir, *Quatermass and the Pit*. Hammer Film Productions, 1967.

Barnfather, Keith, prod, *Return to Devil's End*. Reeltime Pictures, 1993.

Clarke, Alan, dir, *Penda's Fen*. BBC, 1974.

Coppola, Francis Ford, dir, *The Conversation*. Paramount Pictures, 1974.

Eastwood, Clint, dir, *Play Misty for Me*. Universal Pictures, 1971.

Fisher, Terance, dir, *The Devil Rides Out*. Hammer Film Productions, 1968.

Haggard, Piers, dir, *The Blood on Satan's Claw*. Tigon British Film Productions, 1971.

Hardy, Robin, dir, *The Wicker Man*. British Lion Films, 1973.

Myrick, Daniel and Sánchez, Eduardo, dirs., *The Blair Witch Project*. Haxan Films, 1999.

Reeves, Michael, dir, *Witchfinder General*. Tigon British Film Productions, 1968.

Pakula, Alan J., dir, *Klute*. Warner Bros., 1971.

Peckinpah, Sam, dir, *Straw Dogs*. 20th Century Fox, 1971.

Rilla, Wolf, dir, *Village of the Damned*. Metro-Goldwyn-Mayer, 1960.

Siegal, Don, dir, *Invasion of the Body Snatchers*. Walter Wanger Productions, 1956.

Whale, James, dir, *Frankenstein*. Universal Pictures, 1931

Television

The Avengers. ITV/ABC/Thames, 1961-69.

Thingumajig. ITV, 2 April 1969.

Chronicle. BBC, 1966-91.

Silbury Dig:The Heart of the Mound, BBC, 27 July 1968.

Doctor Who: Thirty Years in the TARDIS. BBC, 1993.

A History of Horror. BBC, 2010.

Quatermass II. BBC, 1955.

The Quatermass Experiment. BBC, 1953.

Quatermass and the Pit. BBC, 1958-59.

BIOGRAPHY

Matt Barber is a digital marketing consultant living in Exeter, Devon. He has a BA in Medieval Studies, MA in the History and Literature of Witchcraft and a PhD in Film and Visual Culture, all from the University of Exeter. He has been a **Doctor Who** fan from the moment he accidentally saw *City of Death* when he was three years old. Recently he has written reviews for a variety of magazines and websites including Den of Geek and the British Fantasy Journal, and stories and articles for a number of charity anthologies including *Seasons of War, You and Who Else* and *Whoblique Strategies*. He is also a co-host on the Starburst Magazine Blue Box Podcast, on which he regularly strongly disagrees about things that, on the whole, don't really matter too much.

Coming Soon